THEOLOGICAL POTPOURRI

Book 1

Stephen Mandeville

Copyright © 2024 Stephen Mandeville

All rights reserved

"Scripture taken from HOLY BIBLE, NEW INTERNATIONAL VERSION®. Copyright © 1973, 1978, 1984 by International Bible Society. Used by permission of Zondervan Publishing House." 1
1 The Holy Bible: New International Version, (Grand Rapids, MI: Zondervan, 1984).

Greek New Testament copyright 1963, 1967, 1975, 1983 United Bible Societies.
Morphological Database copyright 1995 GRAMCORD.
English Glosses Copyright 1995 Logos Research Systems, Inc.

No part of this book may be reproduced, or stored in a retrieval system, or transmitted in any form or by any means, electronic, mechanical, photocopying, recording, or otherwise, without express written permission of the publisher.

Cover design by: Stephen Mandeville
Printed in the United States of America

CONTENTS

Title Page
Copyright
Preface
"FAITH IS A CONDUIT! NEW NATURE IS THE GOAL!"   1
"TWO WISDOMS"   6
ENCOURAGEMENT FROM THE GREEK NT – PART I   11
AN ENCOUNTER   13
ENCOURAGEMENT FROM THE GREEK NT – PART II   18
AMERICA LOSES HER BLESSING   20
THE GENETICS EXCUSE   27
ENCOURAGEMENT FROM THE GREEK NT – PART III   33
THE COMING JUDGMENT   36
DOUBLE STANDARD   43
THANKSGIVING   47
INTERNAL LIGHT   50
HIDING ETERNAL LIFE   55
HAVING TROUBLE WITH AN EMPTY PURSE?   60
RIGHTEOUSNESS, DEEDS & WORKS   66
REPENTANCE, CONFESSION AND JUSTIFICATION   71
WHICH ARE YOU?   76
ONLY YOU CAN PREVENT WILDFIRES   86

WHAT BASE ARE YOU ON?	94
ENCOURAGEMENT FROM THE GREEK NT – PART IV	105
THREE TOUCHSTONES OF TRUTH	109
A QUANTUM LEAP IN ILLOGIC.	113
THE LOVE OF GOD	118
HEAD AND HEART KNOWLEDGE.	121
PERSONAL REVIVAL	124
JESUS' LOVE LANGUAGE	126
About The Author	131
Books By This Author	133

PREFACE

One of the challenges of any Minister of the Gospel is to provide a message that minister to every level of maturity. The Apostle Paul mentioned that at one point he could not give a church meat because they were still infants, needing milk. Some Churches solve this by only preaching milk or salvation in Main services and the meat is taught in discipleship classes held at other times. I've contemplated giving my messages labels such as 1) Infant Formula, 2) Ice cream, 3) Meat and potatoes & 4) Choking Hazard. Jesus solved this by only speaking in parables publicly that only the seeking would take the time to think about what he said. Then he explained the deeper things privately to his disciples. The scripture also says do not cast your pearls before swine; those who only want to rip and tear at God's Word with no interest to learn from it. I recognize that this format leaves everything out in the open and the possibility of every kind of reaction.

Christianity is all about coming into a living, daily relationship with our Creator God the Father and His Son Jesus Christ through the indwelling of the Holy Spirit. There will always be some who do not want to be shown the character or God and what he expects of us. Isaiah ran into it in his day...

> Isaiah 30:9–11 (NIV84)
> 9 These are rebellious people, deceitful children,
> children unwilling to listen to the LORD's instruction.
> 10 They say to the seers,
> "See no more visions!"
> and to the prophets,

"Give us no more visions of what is right!
Tell us pleasant things,
prophesy illusions.
11 Leave this way,
get off this path,
and stop confronting us
with the Holy One of Israel!"

It is my intention to continually be pointing people toward a closer walk with God. If you fall, get up, forget what is behind and press toward the High Calling of Jesus Christ. If you struggle, take hold of a brother's or sister's hand. If you are a loner get connected to the Body of Christ in a local Spirit filled body of believers. The list goes on and on. We are in a race and only those who cross the finish line win. It is my prayer and goal that you will start the race, preserver in it, and come to a glorious finish in Jesus Christ.

Blessings, Stephen Mandeville

"FAITH IS A CONDUIT! NEW NATURE IS THE GOAL!"

Many today make faith the goal of the Christian life saying that if you believe you are saved. But that doesn't make sense when Jesus said, not everyone that says, "Lord! Lord!" will enter the Kingdom of God. (Matthew 7:21-23) and then in Luke 6:46 "Why do you call me 'Lord, Lord' and don't do what I say?

Paul wrote to the Ephesians telling them that faith is the conduit that leads to the promises and blessings of God (Grace).

Ephesians 2:8–10 (NIV84) 8 For it is by grace you have been saved, through faith—and this not from yourselves, it is the gift of God— 9 not by works, so that no one can boast. 10 For we are God's workmanship, created in Christ Jesus to do good works, which God prepared in advance for us to do.

It's receiving a gift from God, not just believing in him, and that Gift is life changing. The Holy Spirit is referred to as "the Spirit of Grace" and when we receive that GIFT, He gives us a new nature and a new way of thinking and living as we read His Word. What counts is becoming a New Creation in Christ and giving no room for the old way of living.

Galatians 6:14–15 (NIV84) 14 May I never boast except in the cross of our Lord Jesus Christ, through which the world has been crucified to me, and I to the world. 15 Neither circumcision nor uncircumcision means anything; what counts is a new creation.

New birth gives a person the ability or power to be able to become a Child of God, but we must live it out. Those who go beyond just believing in God into seeking His promises to be fulfilled in their lives will seek the infilling of New Birth in their lives.

> John 1:10-13 (NIV84) 10 He was in the world, and though the world was made through him, the world did not recognize him. 11 He came to that which was his own, but his own did not receive him. 12 Yet to all who received him, to those who believed in his name, he gave the right (Greek; Ability/power) to become children of God— 13 children born not of natural descent, nor of human decision or a husband's will, but born of God.

I spent 25 years of my life believing without having surrendered my life to Christ. The person that led me into a personal relationship with Jesus called me a "Believing non-receiver". The fact of the matter is that we must come to faith before we can ask for the things of God. But faith can immunize use against stepping out and seeking the things of God. Believing there is a gift is not the same as having received it. We need to put our faith into action to receive the things of God. Jesus said it very clearly,

> Luke 11:11-13 (NIV84) 11 "Which of you fathers, if your son asks for a fish, will give him a snake instead? 12 Or if he asks for an egg, will give him a scorpion? 13 If you then, though you are evil, know how to give good gifts to your children, how much more will your Father in heaven give the Holy Spirit to those who ask him!"

New birth is just a beginning point. Faith continues to be the conduit that leads us into God's transforming Grace. He has given us everything we need to not only become one of His kids but to start acting like one.

> 2 Peter 1:3–11 (NIV84) 3 His divine power has given us everything we need for life and godliness through our knowledge of him who called us by his own glory and goodness. 4 Through these he has given us his very great and precious promises, so that through them you may participate in the divine nature and escape the corruption in the world caused by evil desires.
> 5 For this very reason, make every effort to add to your faith goodness; and to goodness, knowledge; 6 and to knowledge, self-control; and to self-control, perseverance; and to perseverance, godliness; 7 and to godliness, brotherly kindness; and to brotherly kindness, love. 8 For if you possess these qualities in increasing measure, they will keep you from being ineffective and unproductive in your knowledge of our Lord Jesus Christ. 9 But if anyone does not have them, he is nearsighted and blind, and has forgotten that he has been cleansed from his past sins.
> 10 Therefore, my brothers, be all the more eager to make your calling and election sure. For if you do these things, you will never fall, 11 and you will receive a rich welcome into the eternal kingdom of our Lord and Savior Jesus Christ.

And that New Creation gives us a desire to obey and follow the Lord. Christians are not people who are just naturally religious but are people who have received a gift that has changed their lives. There are many imposters and that is why Jesus didn't say that you would know them by their confession of faith, but he said, "You will know them by their fruit." It isn't about how much you know but about how much you are known by Him and desire to walk with him. Those who truly know him are concerned about what He thinks are right and wrong and it is revealed in their lives. As Paul said,

> 1 Corinthians 7:19 (NIV84) 19 Circumcision is nothing and uncircumcision is nothing. Keeping God's commands is what

counts.

In the following passages the Apostle John, the Apostle of Love, said that there are only two options if a "Believer" keeps walking in darkness and say they know the Lord. One they are a liar or two they do not live by the truth.

> 1 John 1:5–7 (NIV84) 5 This is the message we have heard from him and declare to you: God is light; in him there is no darkness at all. 6 If we claim to have fellowship with him yet walk in the darkness, we lie and do not live by the truth. 7 But if we walk in the light, as he is in the light, we have fellowship with one another, and the blood of Jesus, his Son, purifies us from all sin.

> 1 John 2:3–6 (NIV84) 3 We know that we have come to know him if we obey his commands. 4 The man who says, "I know him," but does not do what he commands is a liar, and the truth is not in him. 5 But if anyone obeys his word, God's love is truly made complete in him. This is how we know we are in him: 6 whoever claims to live in him must walk as Jesus did.

To say that we know the Lord creates a great obligation in our lives. To say that we know God and keep doing the things that he says he hates in His Word is a great offense to Him. I can't say it better than the Apostle Paul,

> Romans 8:12–14 (NIV84) 12 Therefore, brothers, we have an obligation—but it is not to the sinful nature, to live according to it. 13 For if you live according to the sinful nature, you will die; but if by the Spirit you put to death the misdeeds of the body, you will live, 14 because those who are led by the Spirit of God are sons of God.

In our teaching, preaching and beliefs are we constantly excusing the fleshly nature or are we Ministers of the Spirit giving no opportunity to the flesh? The Goal of the Christian life is to become an overcomer; to be in the World but to not be of it. We are part of a Kingdom whose beauty and purity makes this world look like mud. Let's press on toward the High calling of Jesus Christ.

"TWO WISDOMS"

We can know about the Lord but not walk in his wisdom. We live in a world who's values and desires are strongly influenced by a wisdom that does not come from God. The Apostle James wrote about God's wisdom.

> James 3:17–18 (NIV84) 17 But the wisdom that comes from heaven is first of all pure; then peace-loving, considerate, submissive, full of mercy and good fruit, impartial and sincere. 18 Peacemakers who sow in peace raise a harvest of righteousness.

Living in the wisdom and the ways of God are a high and lofty calling; one that cannot be accomplished without divine help. Only the Spirit of Christ can open the eyes of the bind and begin the process of a transformed life. Love by isn't very nature requires a choice, so God even gave the angels freedom of choice. Satan corrupted the wisdom of God and part of the angels followed him until they were cast out of Heaven. God gave the prophet Ezekiel a message for the King of Tyre who was an embodiment of Satan himself.

> Ezekiel 28:11–19 (NIV84) 11 The word of the LORD came to me: 12 "Son of man, take up a lament concerning the king of Tyre and say to him: 'This is what the Sovereign LORD says:
> " 'You were the model of perfection,
> full of wisdom and perfect in beauty.
> 13   You were in Eden, the garden of God;
> every precious stone adorned you:
> ruby, topaz and emerald,

chrysolite, onyx and jasper, sapphire, turquoise and beryl. Your settings and mountings were made of gold; on the day you were created they were prepared.
14   You were anointed as a guardian cherub, for so I ordained you.
You were on the holy mount of God;
you walked among the fiery stones.
15   You were blameless in your ways
from the day you were created
till wickedness was found in you.
16   Through your widespread trade
you were filled with violence,
and you sinned. So I drove you in disgrace from the mount of God,
and I expelled you, O guardian cherub,
from among the fiery stones. 17 Your heart became proud on account of your beauty, and you corrupted your wisdom because of your splendor. So I threw you to the earth; I made a spectacle of you before kings.
18   By your many sins and dishonest trade
you have desecrated your sanctuaries.
So I made a fire come out from you,
and it consumed you, and I reduced you to ashes on the ground in the sight of all who were watching.
19   All the nations who knew you are appalled at you; you have come to a horrible end and will be no more.'

Satan along with his corrupted wisdom was thrown to the earth where he twists the wisdom of God in greed, self-promotion, lust and all others lusts of the flesh rather than promoting the Spirit. The whole world is under the control of the evil one and only those Born of the Spirit have that control broken.

1 John 5:18–19 (NIV84) 18 We know that anyone born of God does not continue to sin; the one who was born of God keeps him safe, and the evil one cannot harm him. 19 We

know that we are children of God, and that the whole world is under the control of the evil one.

Angels of light and Angels of darkness: When people think of satanic control they think of dark rituals with pentagrams. But the fact of the matter is that he has more control in coming as an angel of light. (II Corinthians 11:14) This world system is focused on his wisdom not the wisdom of God and that is why John wrote to the churches not to love the things of the World.

1 John 2:15-17 (RSV) 15 Do not love the world or the things in the world. If anyone loves the world, love for the Father is not in him. 16 For all that is in the world, the lust of the flesh and the lust of the eyes and the pride of life, is not of the Father but is of the world. 17 And the world passes away, and the lust of it; but he who does the will of God abides forever.

In this passage there are three things mentions: lust of the flesh and the lust of the eyes and the pride of life. The first, the lust of the flesh is living for sensuality, feelings, pleasure; gluttony, immorality and drugs of all types fit into this. That's not to say that there are not any appropriate pleasures in life, but the evil one takes them beyond proper levels. He turns love into lust; the desire to consume, to have, to partake rather than to nurture and care for. Second, the lust of the eyes; this is the collector's dream; having more and more beautify things to feast their eyes upon. It's never enough and they really don't mind who they hurt to get what they want. Third is the Pride of Life. There are two Greek words for Life. One is Zoa which is what makes us alive. The other, the one used here is Bios. It means the things that make up one's life, pride in your position, possessions, and abilities. We live in a world that is always seeking promotions, one-upmanship, to keep up and surpass the Jones rather than to care for your fellowman. You see all of these are a twisting or corrupting of the Wisdom of God. They turn the love of God and man into a self-centered pursuit. The Apostle Paul stated clearly in Galatians how the evil one's wisdom can be broken in your life.

Galatians 5:16–25 (NIV84) 16 So I say, live by the Spirit, and you will not gratify the desires of the sinful nature. 17 For the sinful nature desires what is contrary to the Spirit, and the Spirit what is contrary to the sinful nature. They are in conflict with each other, so that you do not do what you want. 18 But if you are led by the Spirit, you are not under law.
19 The acts of the sinful nature are obvious: sexual immorality, impurity and debauchery; 20 idolatry and witchcraft; hatred, discord, jealousy, fits of rage, selfish ambition, dissensions, factions 21 and envy; drunkenness, orgies, and the like. I warn you, as I did before, that those who live like this will not inherit the kingdom of God.
22 But the fruit of the Spirit is love, joy, peace, patience, kindness, goodness, faithfulness, 23 gentleness and self-control. Against such things there is no law. 24 Those who belong to Christ Jesus have crucified the sinful nature with its passions and desires. 25 Since we live by the Spirit, let us keep in step with the Spirit.

God has proclaimed us all sinners because sin is falling short of the Glory of God. We have all participated in some or all the about fleshly act but the reason that Jesus came was to destroy the Devil's work in our lives, not to excuse it.

1 John 3:7–10 (NIV84) 7 Dear children, do not let anyone lead you astray. He who does what is right is righteous, just as he is righteous. 8 He who does what is sinful is of the devil, because the devil has been sinning from the beginning. The reason the Son of God appeared was to destroy the devil's work. 9 No one who is born of God will continue to sin, because God's seed remains in him; he cannot go on sinning, because he has been born of God. 10 This is how we know who the children of God are and who the children of the devil are: Anyone who does not do what is right is not a child of God; nor is anyone who does not love his brother.

Thanks to modern communication and Hollywood we are being bombarded with Satan's corrupted wisdom that is counter to the wisdom of God. Harley-Davidson has a Motorcycle commercial that says, "The Meek inherit nothing", a clear contradiction of Jesus Words that "The Meek will inherit the Earth." Immorality in every form is portrayed as normal in Desperate Housewives, the Bachelor and Bachelorette, and the newest offering of Pan AM. Jesus taught not to take revenge, but this season "Revenge" is offered up in the Hamptons. The wisdom that is portrayed is the corrupt wisdom of the evil one who controls this world's system and who is only kept is some kind of check by those who turn to God's wisdom and His Word.

Many claim to know Christ but the wisdom they follow is from another place. Whose wisdom are you following this day?

ENCOURAGEMENT FROM THE GREEK NT – PART I

Many focus on faith, but Jesus and the Apostles focused on the faith that leads to repentance and on to conversion. The Goal of faith is a new life in Christ. For those who have taken hold of the promise of the Holy Spirit they find the "Parakleat". Para is a Greek preposition meaning alongside. Kaleo is a verb meaning to call. Thus, the Holy Spirit is the one "called alongside" to distribute the grace of God in correcting, encouraging, and leading us through our Christian life and walk. Through a living faith all the promises are "Yes" to those who are filled with His Spirit. The Apostle Paul writes about this in II Corinthians 1:20-22. And they come with an added blessing as well. He wrote.

> 2 Corinthians 1:20–22 (NIV84) 20 For no matter how many promises God has made, they are "Yes" in Christ. And so through him the "Amen" is spoken by us to the glory of God. 21 Now it is God who makes both us and you stand firm in Christ. He anointed us, 22 set his seal of ownership on us, and put his Spirit in our hearts as a deposit, guaranteeing what is to come.

That extra blessing is found in verse 22. The Greek Word translated in the NIV as "a Deposit" is translated in many other versions as an earnest. The word is representative of paying earnest money down on a house. It's saying that you are sincere about coming back and taking possession of the property and claim it as your own. The Holy Spirit is given to those who Jesus intends to come back and take as his own. Evidence of the Holy Spirit's presence is made known through Spiritual Gifts and Spiritual Fruit, but that is another lesson altogether.

I can't speak for anyone else, but as for myself, I want everything that the Lord has to offer us in this life for our strengthening, encouragement and leading. When you seek the Lord with all of your heart, he promises you will find him. Don't be satisfied with a God who is out there somewhere. Don't Just believe in Him. Meet Him. Seek the Holy One who wants to fill your heart with His presence.

AN ENCOUNTER

I took my wife, Ellen, out to lunch for her birthday. While sitting at the table a man came up to us and introduced himself to us and during the conversation said, "I've been in the Church for 38 years and it's just believing in Jesus and it's a done deal. People make things way to complicated when it's so simple." And then he shook our hands and walked away.

The problem is that relationships are always complicated, and Christianity is about a relationship with God and Christ and the Holy Spirit. I could just believe that Ellen is my wife and never take her out to lunch or interact with her and I wouldn't still have a marriage. Interacting with God is a life changing experience. Jesus didn't say that you would know his people by their confession of faith but by their fruit because to encounter Him affects every area of life. The Apostle John said that anyone who continues to sin and says they know the Father is either a liar or doesn't live by the truth.

Many take the passage where the Apostle Paul says that we are not saved by works to be a license (Licentiousness) to live as you want. But he was talking about the fact that his conversion was a free gift, his actions didn't warrant it. That conversion changed his life and actions forever. Christianity is so much more than just believing. In fact, Jesus said that not everyone that says 'Lord, Lord' will enter the kingdom of God. The Apostle Paul also talked about the effects of that conversion and the necessity to act upon it.

Romans 8:1–8 (NIV84)

> 8   Therefore, there is now no condemnation for those who are in Christ Jesus, 2 because through Christ Jesus the law of the Spirit of life set me free from the law of sin and death. 3 For what the law was powerless to do in that it was weakened by the sinful nature, God did by sending his own Son in the likeness of sinful man to be a sin offering. And so he condemned sin in sinful man, 4 in order that the righteous requirements of the law might be fully met in us, who do not live according to the sinful nature but according to the Spirit.
> 5 Those who live according to the sinful nature have their minds set on what that nature desires; but those who live in accordance with the Spirit have their minds set on what the Spirit desires. 6 The mind of sinful man is death, but the mind controlled by the Spirit is life and peace; 7 the sinful mind is hostile to God. It does not submit to God's law, nor can it do so. 8 Those controlled by the sinful nature cannot please God.

We have an obligation to live a new life through the Spirit of God. Faith of itself is not enough. Many think they can believe in Christ, act like the devil and they will still be accepted by God. Jesus died to change us not continually excuse us. Jesus is not an excuse for evil behavior. The Apostle Paul wrote about that obligation.

> Romans 8:12–14 (NIV84) 12 Therefore, brothers, we have an obligation—but it is not to the sinful nature, to live according to it. 13 For if you live according to the sinful nature, you will die; but if by the Spirit you put to death the misdeeds of the body, you will live, 14 because those who are led by the Spirit of God are sons of God.

Jesus' message was repent for the Kingdom of God is at hand. Many believe without coming to a place of repentance and they do not realize that they are "storing up wrath" for the day of Judgment. It's time the Church wake up and take hold of the power of God to change their own lives and proclaim the message of transformation to the nations.

> Romans 2:5–11 (NIV84) 5 But because of your stubbornness and your unrepentant heart, you are storing up wrath against yourself for the day of God's wrath, when his righteous judgment will be revealed. 6 God "will give to each person according to what he has done." 7 To those who by persistence in doing good seek glory, honor and immortality, he will give eternal life. 8 But for those who are self-seeking and who reject the truth and follow evil, there will be wrath and anger. 9 There will be trouble and distress for every human being who does evil: first for the Jew, then for the Gentile; 10 but glory, honor and peace for everyone who does good: first for the Jew, then for the Gentile. 11 For God does not show favoritism.

This last phrase literally says, "God is not a respecter of persons." Your faith will not save you if you continue in old and sinful ways. God will judge all by the same standards, but the Christians past is wiped away at the point of conversion and only what has been done in Christ will be judged, both wicked and good. The Apostle Peter stated it clearly,

> 1 Peter 4:17–18 (NIV84) 17 For it is time for judgment to begin with the family of God; and if it begins with us, what will the outcome be for those who do not obey the gospel of God? 18 And,
> "If it is hard for the righteous to be saved,
> what will become of the ungodly and the sinner?"

Don't build a belief system on one passage, take it all in. Live for eternity not for the moment, for the scriptures are clear as to the kind of people we ought to be as we live out our lives here.

> 2 Peter 3:11–14 (NIV84) 11 Since everything will be destroyed in this way, what kind of people ought you to be? You ought to live holy and godly lives 12 as you look forward to the day of God and speed its coming. That day

will bring about the destruction of the heavens by fire, and the elements will melt in the heat. 13 But in keeping with his promise we are looking forward to a new heaven and a new earth, the home of righteousness.
14 So then, dear friends, since you are looking forward to this, make every effort to be found spotless, blameless and at peace with him.

It does not matter what our culture approves and accepts. God's Kingdom goes by God's rules. Correction is not a matter of hate but of love, wanting everyone to come to the knowledge of God and the Spirit. Repent and turn to him because a faith that is without a converted, transformed and changed life is worthless.

1 Corinthians 6:9–11 (ESV) 9 Or do you not know that the unrighteous will not inherit the kingdom of God? Do not be deceived: neither the sexually immoral, nor idolaters, nor adulterers, nor men who practice homosexuality, 10 nor thieves, nor the greedy, nor drunkards, nor revilers, nor swindlers will inherit the kingdom of God. 11 And such were some of you. But you were washed, you were sanctified, you were justified in the name of the Lord Jesus Christ and by the Spirit of our God.

People want an impersonal doctrine of belief rather than a relationship that will change them. The Prophet Isaiah found this to be true and it is as true today.

Isaiah 30:9–11 (NIV84)
9 These are rebellious people, deceitful children,
children unwilling to listen to the LORD's instruction.
10 They say to the seers,
"See no more visions!"
and to the prophets,
"Give us no more visions of what is right!
Tell us pleasant things,
prophesy illusions.

11 Leave this way,
get off this path,
and stop confronting us
with the Holy One of Israel!"

We make two mistakes in our handling of our beliefs, and they are the same the Pharisee's made when Jesus confronted them.

Matthew 22:29 (NIV84) 29 Jesus replied, "You are in error because you do not know the Scriptures or the power of God.

We can build a doctrine a belief system on a single passage that contradicts so many others, and really have a Gospel that omits the power of God to change and transform a life. Don't settle for the world. The Kingdom of God has so much more to offer.

ENCOURAGEMENT FROM THE GREEK NT – PART II

Where did the Tutor go? Tutors are necessary until a child becomes competent to live their life as productive and Good Citizens. The Apostle Paul spoke of the Law as a Tutor that prepared the believer for the freedom of that Grace brings. The Passage is as follows:

> Galatians 4:1-7   What I am saying is that as long as the heir is a child, he is no different from a slave, although he owns the whole estate. 2 He is subject to guardians and trustees until the time set by his father. 3 So also, when we were children, we were in slavery under the basic principles of the world. 4 But when the time had fully come, God sent his Son, born of a woman, born under law, 5 to redeem those under law, that we might receive the full rights of sons. 6 Because you are sons, God sent the Spirit of his Son into our hearts, the Spirit who calls out, "Abba, Father." 7 So you are no longer a slave, but a son; and since you are a son, God has made you also an heir.

Paul uses a Greek word that was very common and quickly understood by the people of his day. The Word is Oikonomous, which was a Slave or Servant in a Wealthy Home. He ruled and managed the entire estate for his master. One of his duties was to train and educate the Masters Children. Paul is making the connection between this and the Believer and the Law. The Law is a Nanny or Governess to train us until the time we become mature and can enjoy the freedom of Christian Adulthood.

The Problem is that today we teach our Children the freedom of Grace before we teach them the righteousness of God embodied in the Law. It is the Law that reveals our true need than can only be fulfilled in Christ. As The Apostle said concerning the Law...

Romans 3:31 (NIV84) 31 Do we, then, nullify the law by this faith? Not at all! Rather, we uphold the law.

Romans 7:7 (NIV84) 7 What shall we say, then? Is the law sin? Certainly not! Indeed I would not have known what sin was except through the law. For I would not have known what coveting really was if the law had not said, "Do not covet."

Romans 7:12 (NIV84) 12 So then, the law is holy, and the commandment is holy, righteous and good.

Our children have grown up without a sense of right and wrong and without a concept of sin. The Old Testament was given to prepare us for the New Testament. Many skip the Old Testament all together and really do not know the power of Transformation that the New affords.

Let's find the Tutor again that we may all grow up into the full image of Christ and become Mature Citizens in the Kingdom of God.

AMERICA LOSES HER BLESSING

Two things are mentioned in the scripture that will cause you to lose the blessings of God and eventually keep you out of heaven if you persist in these things: Sexual immorality and Idolatry. This message is focused on sexual immorality.

The fall of many great nations has come on the turn to sexual immorality. It is big business in the United States today.

1. Hollywood and the Women's Movement promote it.

2. The Condom and Birth Control Industry support it.

3. The Abortion industry steps in where the previous fails.

4. The Drug Companies labor to develop drugs that will relieve the effects of Sexually Transmitted Diseases and HIV.

5. And finally there are Social Service Agencies to have the middle class pay for it.

We as a people hate fences. I agree with someone who once said, "Instead of building fences at the top of the cliff, we just build hospitals at the bottom." But the fact of the matter is that freedom comes with a great level of responsibility. Freedom is a very dangerous gift. People can choose to use their freedom for good or evil. The Apostle Peter uses the words Submission and Freedom in the same breath. Unrestrained freedom is anarchy. I live in a free country but there are many laws that protect the freedoms of all.

> 1 Peter 2:13–17 (NIV84) 13 Submit yourselves for the Lord's sake to every authority instituted among men: whether to the king, as the supreme authority, 14 or to governors, who are sent by him to punish those who do wrong and to commend those who do right. 15 For it is God's will that by doing good you should silence the ignorant talk of foolish men. 16 Live as free men, but do not use your freedom as a cover-up for evil; live as servants of God. 17 Show proper respect to everyone: Love the brotherhood of believers, fear God, honor the king.

The women's movement has done a great deal of good in righting wrongs that discriminated against women. But their fight for freedom has gone beyond the bounds of responsibility in moving into an area that is bringing God's Judgment upon this nation. Abortion and a desire for independence has driven the movement into a place that belittles marriage and morality. God's Word says that a man that has sexual relations with a woman outside of marriage defiles her in God's eyes. It also says that Marriage is to be honored by all and the marriage bed is undefiled. The opposite of that statement is that the bed of the unmarried, those living together or one-night stands, is defiled. The Kingdom of God is about God's view of righteousness, not ours. Abstaining from sexual immorality is basic to Christianity.

Hebrews 6 lays out the basic teaching of Christianity:

> Hebrews 6:1-3 (NIV84) Therefore let us leave the elementary teachings about Christ and go on to maturity, not laying again the foundation of repentance from acts that lead to death, and of faith in God, 2 instruction about baptisms, the laying on of hands, the resurrection of the dead, and eternal judgment. 3 And God permitting, we will do so.

Anyone knowing the Old Testament knows what "acts that lead to death" were. There were only a few commands that were not redeemable. These the Lord said, "Their blood will be on their own heads." All sexual acts outside of heterosexual marriage is one of them. When the gospel went out to the Nations (Gentiles) who did not have the Word of God, the Lord even forgave these things but the converted needed to repent for those kinds of acts. Belief in Jesus is not a license to sin (licentiousness) but the reason for a change, converted, transformed life through New Birth.

The Apostle Paul brought about the Jerusalem Council recorded in Acts 15 which laid out the basic requirement that should be proclaimed to the Gentiles (The Nations). Here is the conclusion of the matter.

> Acts 15:28-29 (NIV84) 28 It seemed good to the Holy Spirit and to us not to burden you with anything beyond the following requirements: 29 You are to abstain from food sacrificed to idols, from blood, from the meat of strangled animals and from sexual immorality. You will do well to avoid these things. Farewell.

The Apostle Peter stated how those who put their faith in God should live:

> 1 Peter 2:11-12 (NIV84) 11 Dear friends, I urge you, as aliens and strangers in the world, to abstain from sinful desires, which war against your soul. 12 Live such good lives among the pagans that, though they accuse you of doing wrong, they may see your good deeds and glorify God on the day he visits us.

> Hebrews 13:4 (NIV84) 4 Marriage should be honored by all, and the marriage bed kept pure, for God will judge the adulterer and all the sexually immoral.

Sexual Immorality wars against your soul and blinds you to the things of God. It, in the end, will lead to Judgment. Jesus didn't die just to excuse us but to change us. There is a man who epitomizes what is happening in our country today. In Number 22-24 is the story of Balaam. A king wanted to defeat God's people, so he hired Balaam to curse them. But the Lord would not let Balaam Curse his people keeping the great reward the King offered from Balaam. Finally, Balaam taught the king how to defeat them by turning their God against them by getting them to get involved in immorality and idolatry. Throughout the Scriptures Balaam is recognized as a name that represents defeat and destruction. Jesus, in Revelation 2-3 mentions Balaam several times as well as Jezebel who taught people that sexual immorality was acceptable. Read the final words about Balaam life and legacy.

> Numbers 31:15–16 (NIV84) 15 "Have you allowed all the women to live?" he asked them. 16 "They were the ones who followed Balaam's advice and were the means of turning the Israelites away from the LORD in what happened at Peor, so that a plague struck the LORD's people.

> Revelation 2:14 (NIV84) 14 Nevertheless, I have a few things against you: You have people there who hold to the teaching of Balaam, who taught Balak to entice the Israelites to sin by eating food sacrificed to idols and by committing sexual immorality.

God is long suffering. He hopes people will listen and repent. But if we stubbornly keep going his judgment is going to fall. My heart goes out to all the young ladies who are buying into this philosophy for statistics show they are much more likely to live out their lives in poverty. The greater judgment will be on the Jezebels who are promoting this lifestyle. Jesus made it clear.

> Matthew 18:5–9 (NIV84) 5 "And whoever welcomes a little child like this in my name welcomes me. 6 But if anyone causes one of these little ones who believe in me to sin, it would be better for him to have a large millstone hung around his neck and to be drowned in the depths of the sea.
> 7 "Woe to the world because of the things that cause people to sin! Such things must come, but woe to the man through whom they come! 8 If your hand or your foot causes you to

sin cut it off and throw it away. It is better for you to enter life maimed or crippled than to have two hands or two feet and be thrown into eternal fire. 9 And if your eye causes you to sin, gouge it out and throw it away. It is better for you to enter life with one eye than to have two eyes and be thrown into the fire of hell.

The effect of this will be multiple. God is removing his hand of blessing from this nation and as the number of unwed mothers increase the burden upon the masses to support them in welfare will further cripple this nation. We need to be promoting self-sufficient responsible citizens, not those making their living off of the middle class. But the ultimate effect is that they are turning God against this nation and working to keep people out of the Kingdom of God because said that the sexually immoral shall net enter his Kingdom.

> Revelation 22:11–15 (NIV84) 11 Let him who does wrong continue to do wrong; let him who is vile continue to be vile; let him who does right continue to do right; and let him who is holy continue to be holy."
> 12 "Behold, I am coming soon! My reward is with me, and I will give to everyone according to what he has done. 13 I am the Alpha and the Omega, the First and the Last, the Beginning and the End.
> 14 "Blessed are those who wash their robes, that they may have the right to the tree of life and may go through the gates into the city. 15 Outside are the dogs, those who practice magic arts, the sexually immoral, the murderers, the idolaters and everyone who loves and practices falsehood.

The bottom line is this:

> 2 Chronicles 7:13–14 (NIV84) 13 "When I shut up the heavens so that there is no rain, or command locusts to devour the land or send a plague among my people, 14 if my people, who are called by my name, will humble themselves

and pray and seek my face and turn from their wicked ways, then will I hear from heaven and will forgive their sin and will heal their land.

You can say, well He's not doing anything to me. I'm OK as I live this way. God is longsuffering wishing all to come to repentance but what people do not realize is that they are storing up wrath for that day, and Romans 2 makes it clear.

Romans 2:5–11 (NIV84) 5 But because of your stubbornness and your unrepentant heart, you are storing up wrath against yourself for the day of God's wrath, when his righteous judgment will be revealed. 6 God "will give to each person according to what he has done." 7 To those who by persistence in doing good seek glory, honor and immortality, he will give eternal life. 8 But for those who are self-seeking and who reject the truth and follow evil, there will be wrath and anger. 9 There will be trouble and distress for every human being who does evil: first for the Jew, then for the Gentile; 10 but glory, honor and peace for everyone who does good: first for the Jew, then for the Gentile. 11 For God does not show favoritism.

Repent (turn) for there is a wealth of forgiveness and grace available for those who turn to God. If that is your desire, please pray this simple prayer with a repentant heart and find a good Bible believing Church to help you grow.

Lord, Jesus. I see from your Word that I have sinned. I accept you sacrifice for me today and ask you to come into my heart and life today. Fill me with your Spirit and lead me in the way I should go. I ask this in Jesus Name. Amen.

The Apostle Paul said, "forgetting what is behind, I press on toward the high calling of Jesus Christ. Don't let the enemy of your soul beat you up about the past, but make this a new day in Jesus Christ. Press on."

If you prayed this prayer please get connected with a body of full gospel believers who will bless and encourage you in your walk with Christ. May God Grant You Repentance, in Jesus Name.

THE GENETICS EXCUSE

Sin isn't a popular topic these days. You are supposed to accept everyone as they are. That sounds good on the surface, but the fact of the matter is that not everyone is going to enter the Kingdom of God and as a Pastor I am under commission to point people in that direction. So here we go. When we compare ourselves with one another we can always find someone that will make us look good. But the fact of the matter is that the standard that God uses is himself.

> Romans 3:23 (NIV84) 23 for all have sinned and fall short of the glory of God,

Sin is falling short of God's glory, His purity, His holiness, His love, His Joy, His peace, His Kindness, His selflessness, His peace. You can wear nice clothes and get all slicked up but the fact of the matter is we have all fallen short of His Glory.

Since the fall in the garden of Eden we have, all been oriented to selfishness and satisfying our own flesh rather than living for God as we were originally created to do. Rather than confessing our sin and turning to God, people are always looking for ways to justify their sin. But there is a way that seems right to a man that leads to death. (Proverbs 14:12) Another proverb says is succinctly.

> Proverbs 28:13 (NIV84)
> 13 He who conceals his sins does not prosper,
> but whoever confesses and renounces them finds mercy.

One of the biggest cover-ups in the history of man is used in the excuse of sexual orientation being a matter of DNA. Skin color is a matter of DNA and shouldn't matter in the least, but if our actions are a matter of programming then in reality nothing can be declared right or wrong. It's "Politically Correct" to be a proponent of homosexuality these days but here are some "orientations" that no one is going to look for a DNA link to excuse them.

- Adulterers & Polygamists could have a DNA orientation toward multiple women.
- Thieves could have a DNA orientation toward stealing.
- Dictators could have a DNA orientation toward Controlling.
- The Sexually Immoral could have a DNA orientation toward promiscuity.
- Child Molesters could have a DNA orientation toward Children.
- Murders could have a DNA orientation toward killing.

Is anyone going to try to find a biological link to excuse them? By the way, God was there when we were created and fell from grace and He knows our DNA and still proclaims homosexual activities, as well as those above, as sin that requires death. Romans Chapter 1 gives a different reason for homosexuality.

Romans 1:18–32 (NIV84)
18 The wrath of God is being revealed from heaven against all the godlessness and wickedness of men who suppress the truth by their wickedness, 19 since what may be known about God is plain to them, because God has made it plain to them. 20 For since the creation of the world God's invisible qualities—his eternal power and divine nature—have been clearly seen, being understood from what has been made, so that men are without excuse.
21 For although they knew God, they neither glorified him

as God nor gave thanks to him, but their thinking became futile and their foolish hearts were darkened. 22 Although they claimed to be wise, they became fools 23 and exchanged the glory of the immortal God for images made to look like mortal man and birds and animals and reptiles.

24 Therefore God gave them over in the sinful desires of their hearts to sexual impurity for the degrading of their bodies with one another. 25 They exchanged the truth of God for a lie, and worshiped and served created things rather than the Creator—who is forever praised. Amen.

26 Because of this, God gave them over to shameful lusts. Even their women exchanged natural relations for unnatural ones. 27 In the same way the men also abandoned natural relations with women and were inflamed with lust for one another. Men committed indecent acts with other men, and received in themselves the due penalty for their perversion.

28 Furthermore, since they did not think it worthwhile to retain the knowledge of God, he gave them over to a depraved mind, to do what ought not to be done. 29 They have become filled with every kind of wickedness, evil, greed and depravity. They are full of envy, murder, strife, deceit and malice. They are gossips, 30 slanderers, God-haters, insolent, arrogant and boastful; they invent ways of doing evil; they disobey their parents; 31 they are senseless, faithless, heartless, ruthless. 32 Although they know God's righteous decree that those who do such things deserve death, they not only continue to do these very things but also approve of those who practice them.

In this passage is says over and again "God gave them over". Did he change their DNA? How did He do that? It doesn't say. But God does give people over to their lust if they persist in rejecting the things of God. They suppress the truth. They exchanged the truth of God for a lie. They do not consider it worthwhile to retain the knowledge of God. There is a spiritual component here rather than a physical one. And those with stubborn unrepentant hearts are storing up wrath for the Day of Judgment. Romans Chapter 2 says that they are storing up wrath for that day:

> Romans 2:5–9 (NIV84) 5 But because of your stubbornness and your unrepentant heart, you are storing up wrath against yourself for the day of God's wrath, when his righteous judgment will be revealed. 6 God "will give to each person according to what he has done." 7 To those who by persistence in doing good seek glory, honor and immortality, he will give eternal life. 8 But for those who are self-seeking and who reject the truth and follow evil, there will be wrath and anger. 9 There will be trouble and distress for every human being who does evil: first for the Jew, then for the Gentile;

But thanks be to God He has devised a way for us to be reoriented towards Him through the "Renewing" of New Birth. To change us takes a radical reconstruction of our inner person called New Birth. Jesus made it clear.

> John 3:4–9 (NIV84) 4 "How can a man be born when he is old?" Nicodemus asked. "Surely he cannot enter a second time into his mother's womb to be born!"
> 5 Jesus answered, "I tell you the truth, no one can enter the kingdom of God unless he is born of water and the Spirit. 6 Flesh gives birth to flesh, but the Spirit gives birth to spirit. 7 You should not be surprised at my saying, 'You must be born again.' 8 The wind blows wherever it pleases. You hear its sound, but you cannot tell where it comes from or where it is going. So it is with everyone born of the Spirit."
> 9 "How can this be?" Nicodemus asked.

> Luke 18:17 (NIV84) 17 I tell you the truth, anyone who will not receive the kingdom of God like a little child will never enter it."

When a person is born again all things become new and the Word of God comes to life. You look at the World and Life differently.

> 2 Corinthians 5:17 (AV) 17 Therefore if any man be in Christ, he is a new creature: old things are passed away; behold, all things are become new.

My son said to me just the other day, "People worry about what they must give up, and you do have to give up things. But they don't realize how much of a new world opens to you when you finally do it."

Renewal:

> Colossians 3:5–11 (RSV) 5 Put to death therefore what is earthly in you: fornication, impurity, passion, evil desire, and covetousness, which is idolatry. 6 On account of these the wrath of God is coming. 7 In these you once walked, when you lived in them. 8 But now put them all away: anger, wrath, malice, slander, and foul talk from your mouth. 9 Do not lie to one another, seeing that you have put off the old nature with its practices 10 and have put on the new nature, which is being renewed in knowledge after the image of its creator. 11 Here there cannot be Greek and Jew, circumcised and uncircumcised, barbarian, Scythian, slave, free man, but Christ is all, and in all.

Transformation:

> Romans 12:2 (RSV) 2 Do not be conformed to this world but be transformed by the renewal of your mind, that you may prove what is the will of God, what is good and acceptable and perfect.

The Greek word used for "transformed" is metamorphosis. It's a complete changing of orientation from one form of life to another. Some people think that there are those who are just religiously oriented, but none of us are. True Christians have been changed, renewed, transformed from their former way of live and they know and see the difference that Christ has made in their lives.

This gift of reorientation only comes through asking the Spirit of Jesus Christ to come into your life and forgive your sins as your turn toward Him and His ways.

> Luke 11:9-13 (NIV84) 9 "So I say to you: Ask and it will be given to you; seek and you will find; knock and the door will be opened to you. 10 For everyone who asks receives; he who seeks finds; and to him who knocks, the door will be opened.
> 11 "Which of you fathers, if your son asks for a fish, will give him a snake instead? 12 Or if he asks for an egg, will give him a scorpion? 13 If you then, though you are evil, know how to give good gifts to your children, how much more will your Father in heaven give the Holy Spirit to those who ask him!"

Repent (turn) for there is a wealth of forgiveness and grace available for those who turn to God. If that is your desire, please pray this simple prayer with a repentant heart and find a good, Full Gospel, Bible believing Church to help you grow. Pray the following to Jesus,

"Lord, Jesus. I see from your Word that I have sinned. I accept you sacrifice for me today and ask you to come into my heart and life today. Fill me with your Spirit, renew me, transform me and lead me in the way I should go. I ask this in Jesus Name. Amen."

The Apostle Paul said, "Forgetting what is behind, I press on toward the high calling of Jesus Christ. Don't let the enemy of your soul beat you up about the past but make this a new day in Jesus Christ. Press on."

If you prayed this prayer, please get connected with a body of Full Gospel believers who will bless and encourage you in your walk with Christ. May God Grant You Repentance, in Jesus Name.

ENCOURAGEMENT FROM THE GREEK NT – PART III

Prayer! It's our communication to God. The Father establishes the link whenever anyone turns to His Son Jesus Christ. God answers every prayer. Yes, No, and it depends, are all answers. Now we are going to look at James' correction to the Church in how they prayed. How would you like to see more of your prayers answered in the affirmative? Let's look at …

> James 4:1–6 (NIV84) 4 What causes fights and quarrels among you? Don't they come from your desires that battle within you? 2 You want something but don't get it. You kill and covet, but you cannot have what you want. You quarrel and fight. You do not have, because you do not ask God. 3 When you ask, you do not receive, because you ask with wrong motives, that you may spend what you get on your pleasures.
> 4 You adulterous people, don't you know that friendship with the world is hatred toward God? Anyone who chooses to be a friend of the world becomes an enemy of God. 5 Or do you think Scripture says without reason that the spirit he caused to live in us envies intensely? 6 But he gives us more grace. That is why Scripture says:
> "God opposes the proud
> but gives grace to the humble."

I've underlined the section that I will be focusing on today. In this section the word "ask" appears three times. In it James seems to contradict himself because he says you do not ask and then say when you ask. There is a little piece of Greek Grammar here that is very important. In English we have two "voices". The active voice (I threw the ball) and the passive voice (The boy threw the ball). That's it. But in Greek there is another voice. The Middle voice. The middle voice means the action of the verb is being done with strong personal interest. Let's look at that section again adding the middle voice.

> You do not have, because you do not ask (with strong personal interest) God. 3 When you ask (with strong personal interest), you do not receive, because you ask with wrong motives, that you may spend what you get on your pleasures.

"You do not have, because you do not ask with strong personal interest." I call these Baseball prayers. "Hey God, Catch!" We've all done them. We are going along, and we remember something we wanted to pray about or something someone else asked us to pray about and we say, "Oh yah God, remember so or so!" or "Oh ya God, about giving me this or that." And then we are on about our business. Baseball prayers. The Lord is a personal God, and he likes interaction not just playing catch one way communication.

We can all be passionate when it's something we want but are we as passionate about prayer when it comes to someone else. That brings us to the second part of this section, "When you ask with strong personal interest, you do not receive, because you ask with wrong motives, that you may spend what you get on your pleasures." When we want something, we can pray with strong personal interest. Do we pray the same way when it someone else who wants something?

The kind of prayer that God likes is when we are praying for one another, concerned about each other's needs and wants. God doesn't like self-centered and greedy prayers. When we pray for one another, we balance each other out and we ask for things that are not the kinds of things God is not going to give. God loves a caring and loving heart. Want more prayers answered? Ask a brother or sister in Christ to pray for you. If it's something that you would be ashamed to ask them to pray for, it's also something you shouldn't be asking God for. James ends this section some strong words:

4 You adulterous people, don't you know that friendship with the world is hatred toward God? Anyone who chooses to be a friend of the world becomes an enemy of God.

If the only time we talk to the Lord is to get something for our pleasure, He sees a prayer that is in love with the world. Pray with passion for one another's needs and wants and you will see more "Yes!" answers to your prayers. Better yet, pray for the souls of lost men and women and children who need Jesus Christ as their Lord and Savior.

THE COMING JUDGMENT

Most do not want to hear, or think about, God's coming judgment. The fact of the matter is that Jesus died on the cross to make a way to avoid it. The judgment is coming not because God is mean but because he is Holy and Pure and Clean. He promises a time when He will remove all such things from this earth. He has provided a way. Please take it. The way is by coming into a relationship with Jesus through new birth. What I am about to share is not something I have made up but is taken from statements made by Jesus Christ and His Apostles. Two Graphic warning from the Old Testament make clear what that Day will be like:

> AMOS 5:18-20 Woe to you who long for the day of the LORD! Why do you long for the day of the LORD? That day will be darkness, not light. 19 It will be as though a man fled from a lion only to meet a bear, as though he entered his house and rested his hand on the wall only to have a snake bite him. 20 Will not the day of the LORD be darkness, not light-- pitch-dark, without a ray of brightness?

> ZEPHANIAH 1:14-2:3 "The great day of the LORD is near-- near and coming quickly. Listen! The cry on the day of the LORD will be bitter, the shouting of the warrior there. 15 That day will be a day of wrath, a day of distress and anguish, a day of trouble and ruin, a day of darkness and gloom, a day of clouds and blackness, 16 a day of trumpet and battle cry against the fortified cities and against the corner towers.

17 I will bring distress on the people and they will walk like blind men, because they have sinned against the LORD. Their blood will be poured out like dust and their entrails like filth. 18 Neither their silver nor their gold will be able to save them on the day of the LORD'S wrath. In the fire of his jealousy the whole world will be consumed, for he will make a sudden end of all who live in the earth." 2:1 Gather together, gather together, O shameful nation, 2 before the appointed time arrives and that day sweeps on like chaff, before the fierce anger of the LORD comes upon you, before the day of the LORD'S wrath comes upon you. 3 Seek the LORD, all you humble of the land, you who do what he commands. Seek righteousness, seek humility; perhaps you will be sheltered on the day of the LORD'S anger.

Jesus made it very clear that without New Birth no one will enter the Kingdom of God. You must ask the Spirit of God into your life in order to begin the preparatory work of becoming ready for Heaven.

John 3:5–8 (NIV84) 5 Jesus answered, "I tell you the truth, no one can enter the kingdom of God unless he is born of water and the Spirit. 6 Flesh gives birth to flesh, but the Spirit gives birth to spirit. 7 You should not be surprised at my saying, 'You must be born again.' 8 The wind blows wherever it pleases. You hear its sound, but you cannot tell where it comes from or where it is going. So it is with everyone born of the Spirit."

Jesus and his forerunner, John the Baptist, also said that you will know them by their fruit, not by their confession of faith. A person that has been born again will show the evidence of turning to what God says is right, not what our culture accepts and approves. A tree is known by it's fruit. John the Baptist said.

Matthew 3:7–10 (NIV84) 7 But when he saw many of the Pharisees and Sadducees coming to where he was baptizing, he said to them: "You brood of vipers! Who warned you to flee from the coming wrath? 8 Produce fruit in keeping with repentance. 9 And do not think you can say to yourselves, 'We have Abraham as our father.' I tell you that out of these stones God can raise up children for Abraham. 10 The ax is already at the root of the trees, and every tree that does not produce good fruit will be cut down and thrown into the fire.

Jesus confirmed what he said in His teaching.

Matthew 12:33-37 (NIV84) 33 "Make a tree good and its fruit will be good, or make a tree bad and its fruit will be bad, for a tree is recognized by its fruit. 34 You brood of vipers, how can you who are evil say anything good? For out of the overflow of the heart the mouth speaks. 35 The good man brings good things out of the good stored up in him, and the evil man brings evil things out of the evil stored up in him. 36 But I tell you that men will have to give account on the day of judgment for every careless word they have spoken. 37 For by your words you will be acquitted, and by your words you will be condemned."

Jesus told a parable that states that after a man receives the Spirit, He is given time to start producing fruit, but if he does not dire consequences may take place.

Luke 13:6-9 (NIV84) 6 Then he told this parable: "A man had a fig tree, planted in his vineyard, and he went to look for fruit on it, but did not find any. 7 So he said to the man who took care of the vineyard, 'For three years now I've been coming to look for fruit on this fig tree and haven't found any. Cut it down! Why should it use up the soil?'
8 "'Sir,' the man replied, 'leave it alone for one more year, and I'll dig around it and fertilize it. 9 If it bears fruit next year, fine! If not, then cut it down.'"

Jesus drew a line in the sand for the level of fruitfulness he expects to see in those who receive him. And personally, I believe

THEOLOGICAL POTPOURRI

He meant what he said. Men develop doctrines that say once saved always saved, but there are too many passages that show God's Judgment will be upon those who do not produce spiritual fruit.

> Matthew 5:17–20 (NIV84) 17 "Do not think that I have come to abolish the Law or the Prophets; I have not come to abolish them but to fulfill them. 18 I tell you the truth, until heaven and earth disappear, not the smallest letter, not the least stroke of a pen, will by any means disappear from the Law until everything is accomplished. 19 Anyone who breaks one of the least of these commandments and teaches others to do the same will be called least in the kingdom of heaven, but whoever practices and teaches these commands will be called great in the kingdom of heaven. 20 For I tell you that unless your righteousness surpasses that of the Pharisees and the teachers of the law, you will certainly not enter the kingdom of heaven.

Jesus clearly said that not everyone who says "Lord, Lord" will enter the Kingdom of God. Many use Jesus as an excuse for sinful living rather than the means of a changed and transformed life that New Birth provides.

> Matthew 7:21–23 (NIV84) 21 "Not everyone who says to me, 'Lord, Lord,' will enter the kingdom of heaven, but only he who does the will of my Father who is in heaven. 22 Many will say to me on that day, 'Lord, Lord, did we not prophesy in your name, and in your name drive out demons and perform many miracles?' 23 Then I will tell them plainly, 'I never knew you. Away from me, you evildoers!'

The Apostle Paul lamented over those who live as enemies of the Cross of Christ. Paul wrote that it was not by works that we are saved and many grab hold of that alone. But the Apostle Paul's had a strong conversion theology. It wasn't works that saved him but a powerful life changing experience with Jesus Christ that caused him to press toward the mark of the High Calling of Jesus

Christ. He lamented over those who were not responding to their heavenly calling.

> Philippians 3:18–19 (NIV84) 18 For, as I have often told you before and now say again even with tears, many live as enemies of the cross of Christ. 19 Their destiny is destruction, their god is their stomach, and their glory is in their shame. Their mind is on earthly things.

We who teach shall stand a stricter judgment. I do not live my life for the moment but for that day when I will stand before God and give an account for my teaching. There will be many teachers whose students will ask them on that day, "Why didn't you warn me?" Many Pastors in churches must soften the Gospel to keep people coming to hear pleasing messages. Salvation is necessary to be prepared for the coming wrath. Teachers and preachers will stand in the front of the Judgment line.

> James 3:1–2 (NIV84) 3 Not many of you should presume to be teachers, my brothers, because you know that we who teach will be judged more strictly. 2 We all stumble in many ways. If anyone is never at fault in what he says, he is a perfect man, able to keep his whole body in check.

> Matthew 5:19 19 Anyone who breaks one of the least of these commandments and teaches others to do the same will be called least in the kingdom of heaven, but whoever practices and teaches these commands will be called great in the kingdom of heaven.

Many people think that I'm OK because I believe, but God's judgments will be impartial. God's judgments are without favoritism. The exact Greek words are that He is not "a respecter of persons".

> 1 Peter 1:17 (NIV84) 17 Since you call on a Father who judges each man's work impartially, live your lives as strangers here in reverent fear.

Colossians 3:23–25 (NIV84) 23 Whatever you do, work at it with all your heart, as working for the Lord, not for men, 24 since you know that you will receive an inheritance from the Lord as a reward. It is the Lord Christ you are serving. 25 Anyone who does wrong will be repaid for his wrong, and there is no favoritism.

Matthew 7:24–27 (NIV84) 24 "Therefore everyone who hears these words of mine and puts them into practice is like a wise man who built his house on the rock. 25 The rain came down, the streams rose, and the winds blew and beat against that house; yet it did not fall, because it had its foundation on the rock. 26 But everyone who hears these words of mine and does not put them into practice is like a foolish man who built his house on sand. 27 The rain came down, the streams rose, and the winds blew and beat against that house, and it fell with a great crash."

Each will be given according to what he has done. If we have neglected so great a salvation we will be accounted a place with non-believers, storing up wrath for that day.

Romans 2:5–11 (NIV84) 5 But because of your stubbornness and your unrepentant heart, you are storing up wrath against yourself for the day of God's wrath, when his righteous judgment will be revealed. 6 God "will give to each person according to what he has done." 7 To those who by persistence in doing good seek glory, honor and immortality, he will give eternal life. 8 But for those who are self-seeking and who reject the truth and follow evil, there will be wrath and anger. 9 There will be trouble and distress for every human being who does evil: first for the Jew, then for the Gentile; 10 but glory, honor and peace for everyone who does good: first for the Jew, then for the Gentile. 11 For God does not show favoritism.

Judgment begins with the People of God, so we should live

like we know him, not as those who do not.

> 1 Peter 4:17–18 (NIV84) 17 For it is time for judgment to begin with the family of God; and if it begins with us, what will the outcome be for those who do not obey the gospel of God? 18 And,
> "If it is hard for the righteous to be saved,
> what will become of the ungodly and the sinner?"

Live for the Lord in a way that is pleasing to Him. The only way you can do that is by entering into a personal relationship with Him. Let's end with Jesus Charge to all that would follow Him.

> Luke 9:23–26 (NIV84) 23 Then he said to them all: "If anyone would come after me, he must deny himself and take up his cross daily and follow me. 24 For whoever wants to save his life will lose it, but whoever loses his life for me will save it. 25 What good is it for a man to gain the whole world, and yet lose or forfeit his very self? 26 If anyone is ashamed of me and my words, the Son of Man will be ashamed of him when he comes in his glory and in the glory of the Father and of the holy angels.

DOUBLE STANDARD

Jesus responded differently to the lost than he did to those who claimed to know God. There was and is a double standard. Let's look at those who have not come to Christ first.

The Apostle Paul referred to himself as the worst of sinners in that he went out, with letters from the religious leaders, to persecute and destroy the Church. He was a murderer, and many innocent people lost their lives at his hand. But when he was confronted with Christ he repented and was forgiven and called to build what he once destroyed. Here are the Apostle Paul's own words about himself.

> 1 Timothy 1:15–16 (NIV84) 15 Here is a trustworthy saying that deserves full acceptance: Christ Jesus came into the world to save sinners—of whom I am the worst. 16 But for that very reason I was shown mercy so that in me, the worst of sinners, Christ Jesus might display his unlimited patience as an example for those who would believe on him and receive eternal life.

Jesus showed incredible mercy and forgiveness to the Woman at the well, the woman caught in adultery and to a host of others throughout history right down to me. He's not looking for you to be good enough, He's looking for you to accept Him into your life and repent, turning toward his ways.

The rub comes into the picture in that many "Christians" think that the same standard that applied to them as unsaved applies to them as saved. But the fact of the matter is that we have an obligation to walk with God. The Apostle Paul said it clearly to the Romans.

> Romans 8:12–14 (NIV84) 12 Therefore, brothers, we have an obligation—but it is not to the sinful nature, to live according to it. 13 For if you live according to the sinful nature, you will die; but if by the Spirit you put to death the misdeeds of the body, you will live, 14 because those who are led by the Spirit of God are sons of God.

In the scriptures there is an old English word that many do not understand today, and few take the time to find out what it means. The word is debauchery. The Greek word that it is translated from means Licentiousness. Licentiousness is looking at the Gospel as a license to sin. As a pastor I cannot even begin to tell you how many times I have had people tell me, "Well, God will forgive me!" This is the licentious spirit. It is planning to sin, knowing its wrong in God's sight, but just figuring that He will forgive anyhow. They see Jesus' work on the cross as a license to continue to live in the old way. Jesus is not an excuse for wicked living but the reason for a changed and transformed life.

Jesus wiped the slate clean for our past sins. From the moment that you ask Christ into your life you are clean in his sight. From that point on we are to walk with God and produce fruit in keeping with repentance. The Apostle Peter spoke of our past sin being forgiven and the need to add to our faith the fruit of the spirit so that we will not be ineffective in our walk with Christ.

> 2 Peter 1:5–9 (NIV84) 5 For this very reason, make every effort to add to your faith goodness; and to goodness, knowledge; 6 and to knowledge, self-control; and to self-control, perseverance; and to perseverance, godliness; 7 and to godliness, brotherly kindness; and to brotherly kindness, love. 8 For if you possess these qualities in increasing measure, they will keep you from being ineffective and unproductive in your knowledge of our Lord Jesus Christ. 9 But if anyone does not have them, he is nearsighted and

blind, and has forgotten that he has been cleansed from his past sins.

Jesus confronted the religious leaders of his day and those who claimed to be able to spiritually see. The double standard and our obligations are clear in Jesus' words.

John 9:39–41 (NIV84) 39 Jesus said, "For judgment I have come into this world, so that the blind will see and those who see will become blind."
40 Some Pharisees who were with him heard him say this and asked, "What? Are we blind too?"
41 Jesus said, "If you were blind, you would not be guilty of sin; but now that you claim you can see, your guilt remains.

The Apostle Paul's heart was torn by the attitude of many that he saw, for they lived as enemies of the cross of Christ. Anyone with a licentious attitude will do so. Here are Paul's words.

Philippians 3:17–19 (NIV84) 17 Join with others in following my example, brothers, and take note of those who live according to the pattern we gave you. 18 For, as I have often told you before and now say again even with tears, many live as enemies of the cross of Christ. 19 Their destiny is destruction, their god is their stomach, and their glory is in their shame. Their mind is on earthly things.

Does this mean that a true Christian can never sin and will be held accountable for everything that happens after they come to Christ? It's a matter of attitude. A true Christian wants to live for the Lord, not excuse their behavior. They hunger and thirst after righteousness and for them there is an advocate. True Christians don't excuse their sin, they take it to Christ and turn from it.

1 John 1:5–2:2 (NIV84) 5 This is the message we have heard from him and declare to you: God is light; in him there is no darkness at all. 6 If we claim to have fellowship with him yet

walk in the darkness, we lie and do not live by the truth. 7 But if we walk in the light, as he is in the light, we have fellowship with one another, and the blood of Jesus, his Son, purifies us from all sin.

8 If we claim to be without sin, we deceive ourselves and the truth is not in us. 9 If we confess our sins, he is faithful and just and will forgive us our sins and purify us from all unrighteousness. 10 If we claim we have not sinned, we make him out to be a liar and his word has no place in our lives.

2   My dear children, I write this to you so that you will not sin. But if anybody does sin, we have one who speaks to the Father in our defense—Jesus Christ, the Righteous One. 2 He is the atoning sacrifice for our sins, and not only for ours but also for the sins of the whole world.

Let us put off the licentious attitude of the sinful and the put on the fruit of the converted and transformed. You can't do this in yourself, it takes the work of the Holy Spirit in your life. Ask Him into your heart today; what you lose will be nothing in comparison to what you gain.

THANKSGIVING

We live in very busy times. My children are almost 30 and 28 and the youngest is 23. They are all young adults with active lifestyles. Trying to find a date to get together for Thanksgiving has become an exercise in high-level planning skills. This year we are having 18 people over to our house for Thanksgiving today after service. With all the rush and preparations, it isn't hard to bypass the time it takes to be truly thankful. A favorite passage of mine on thanksgiving is found in the Psalms.

> Psalm 50:23 (NIV84)
> 23 He who sacrifices thank offerings honors me,
> and he prepares the way
> so that I may show him the salvation of God."
> A variant reading is:
> Psalm 50:23 (NIV84 - Variation)
> 23 He who sacrifices thank offerings honors me,
> and he who considers his way
> I will show the salvation of God."

Both readings are consistent with the Character of God's Word. We will consider both. First let's look at the NIV translation.

Thankfulness prepares the way for God to work in a person's life. Conversely, thanklessness cuts off the blessings of God. We are so busy as a culture, and in this economy, acquiring things that we do not take the time to be thankful for what we have, for the people that are in our lives, and to the God that loved us so much that He sent His Son to pay the price for our redemption. Watching the things reported in the news that happened on "Black Friday" shows greed more than thankfulness. A woman actually used pepper spray to keep other shoppers at bay so she could get what she wanted. Shocking.

Without the Acknowledgement of God, you cannot be truly thankful in the way that opens up God's blessings in your life.

> Proverbs 3:5–6 (NIV84)
> 5 Trust in the LORD with all your heart
> and lean not on your own understanding;
> 6 in all your ways acknowledge him,
> and he will make your paths straight.

For the Christian, Thankfulness should be an everyday occurrence. And it comes as we have eyes to see His hand and leading in our lives. This is where the variant reading comes in.

> Psalm 50:23 (NIV84 - Variation)
> 23 He who sacrifices thank offerings honors me,
> and he who considers his way
> I will show the salvation of God."

Taking the time to consider your way takes meditation and knowing God's Word. When we are Thankful, acknowledging God's hand in our lives and considering the way we live we have discovered a recipe for blessing, leading and joy in our lives. Wither in plenty or want we have the Lord's provision and goodness working within us that produces a peace and joy the World cannot know apart from Him.

I want to take a moment to be thankful. I'm thankful for a God who loved me when I did not love him and took extraordinary measures to bring me to himself through His Son and His Spirit. I am thankful for a loving and godly wife in Ellen. She brings me nothing but good. I'm thankful for two wonderful parents who I love with all my heart. I'm thankful for three children, Leah, Josh, and Nate, who keep our lives from being boring: never a dull moment. I'm thankful for the people our Children have brought into our lives, John, Mattie, Hollie, LeAnn, and Mandi. I'm thankful for my grandkids, Chloe, Chaya, Donte', Mattie and Hollie and Mercedes, who have reminded grandpa that a pillow fight on a Saturday afternoon is a worthwhile use of time. I'm thankful for other ministers and their families who challenge and love me. Thank you, fellow pastors for being godly and passionate people I respect and love. As I look at this list, I realize that the things that I'm thankful for are not things at all. They are people! Things are to be used. People are to be cherished. Thank you, Jesus, for all the people you have brought into my life.

    Will you prepare the way for the blessings of God in your life by considering your way, acknowledging, and thanking God. I hope you will.

INTERNAL LIGHT

It has been a wonderful time as I took a break during the Christmas holiday to focus on family and Friends. I feel led to write today on the Christ that came at Christmas and who he was and what his purpose is.

The Apostle Paul as well as the Twelve looked at Jesus from a Worldly point of view. Without the Holy Spirit they could do no other thing. Plus, Jesus humanity was right before them on a daily basis. He was hungry, got tired and dealt with all the everyday problems of life that we all do. But his words; they were a different thing. The Apostle Paul wrote of his worldly point of view about Christ and the change it made once he had received him.

2 Corinthians 5:15–17 (NIV84) 15 And he died for all, that those who live should no longer live for themselves but for him who died for them and was raised again.

16 So from now on we regard no one from a worldly point of view. Though we once regarded Christ in this way, we do so no longer. 17 Therefore, if anyone is in Christ, he is a new creation; the old has gone, the new has come!

The Apostle John revealed his new vision of who Jesus was in the introductions to be I John and the Gospel of John. Let's start with I John.

1 John 1:1–4 (NIV84) That **which** was from the beginning, **which** we have heard, **which** we have seen with our eyes, **which** we have looked at and our hands have touched—this we proclaim concerning the Word of life. 2 The life appeared;

we have seen it and testify to it, and we proclaim to you the eternal life, **which** was with the Father and has appeared to us. 3 We proclaim to you what we have seen and heard, so that you also may have fellowship with us. And our fellowship is with the Father and with his Son, Jesus Christ. 4 We write this to make our joy complete.

The **Bold Highlighted** words all refer to the same thing. "That Which" is in the neuter form, not masculine. John is looking through the flesh of Jesus and seeing the Eternal life that resided within him. It was that eternal life that was in and with the Father from the very beginning of time. John uses the strong forms in the Greek concerning his contact with this eternal life; "We gazed upon it. We fondled it, we intently listened to it. John was seeing Jesus with eyes that were not from a worldly point of view.

John does it again in the beginning of his Gospel. Jesus is the incarnate Word of God. His Words were not the words of men but the very Word of God. A living Word. Jesus also contained the life. And that life was the light of men.

John 1:1–5 (NIV84)   In the beginning was the Word, and the Word was with God, and the Word was God. 2 He was with God in the beginning.

3 Through him all things were made; without him nothing was made that has been made. 4 In him was life, and that life was the light of men. 5 The light shines in the darkness, but the darkness has not understood it.

That life was the light of men. It's not enough just to believe in Jesus, his life must reside in you. It is only His life that gives light to the inner man. Jesus said that not everyone that says, "Lord, Lord" will enter the Kingdom of God because they were always learning but never coming to a knowledge of the truth, which is Christ in you, the hope of Glory.

A love for darkness is the very thing that hinders us. We all know John 3:16 but few go on to quote John 3:19-21.

> John 3:19–21 (NIV84) 19 This is the verdict: Light has come into the world, but men loved darkness instead of light because their deeds were evil. 20 Everyone who does evil hates the light, and will not come into the light for fear that his deeds will be exposed. 21 But whoever lives by the truth comes into the light, so that it may be seen plainly that what he has done has been done through God."

A love for darkness keeps out the light. He is the Word and his Word and Life are the light of men. But men want a savior, not a transformer. They want the light while holding onto darkness and are hindered in their spiritual advancement. This is the issue even within God's Church. There are those moving forward in leaps and bounds as they expel the darkness in their lives with a passion for living for Christ. But, with Paul, I say with tears, there are far to many who hold onto the darkness rather than letting the light of Christ shine deep into the recesses of their hearts. They are defeated, without Joy and Freedom from sin. Jesus said it plainly.

> Luke 11:33–36 (NIV84) 33 "No one lights a lamp and puts it in a place where it will be hidden, or under a bowl. Instead he puts it on its stand, so that those who come in may see the light. 34 Your eye is the lamp of your body. When your eyes are good, your whole body also is full of light. But when they are bad, your body also is full of darkness. 35 See to it, then, that the light within you is not darkness. 36 Therefore, if your whole body is full of light, and no part of it dark, it will be completely lighted, as when the light of a lamp shines on you."

We need to examine our hearts and make sure we are keeping the Light and Word of Christ aflame in our hearts. Listen to the Holy Spirit urgings and watch our hearts for out of it come the issues of life.

2 Timothy 1:6–7 (NIV84) 6 For this reason I remind you to fan into flame the gift of God, which is in you through the laying on of my hands. 7 For God did not give us a spirit of timidity, but a spirit of power, of love and of self-discipline.

We need to rid ourselves and make sure we are not involved in the "Deeds of Darkness".

Romans 13:12–14 (NIV84) 12 The night is nearly over; the day is almost here. So let us put aside the deeds of darkness and put on the armor of light. 13 Let us behave decently, as in the daytime, not in orgies and drunkenness, not in sexual immorality and debauchery, not in dissension and jealousy. 14 Rather, clothe yourselves with the Lord Jesus Christ, and do not think about how to gratify the desires of the sinful nature.

Ephesians 5:3–21 (NIV84) 3 But among you there must not be even a hint of sexual immorality, or of any kind of impurity, or of greed, because these are improper for God's holy people. 4 Nor should there be obscenity, foolish talk or coarse joking, which are out of place, but rather thanksgiving. 5 For of this you can be sure: No immoral, impure or greedy person—such a man is an idolater—has any inheritance in the kingdom of Christ and of God. 6 Let no one deceive you with empty words, for because of such things God's wrath comes on those who are disobedient. 7 Therefore do not be partners with them.

8 For you were once darkness, but now you are light in the Lord. Live as children of light 9 (for the fruit of the light consists in all goodness, righteousness and truth) 10 and find out what pleases the Lord. 11 Have nothing to do with the fruitless deeds of darkness, but rather expose them. 12 For it is shameful even to mention what the disobedient do in secret. 13 But everything exposed by the light becomes

visible, 14 for it is light that makes everything visible. This is why it is said:

"Wake up, O sleeper,

rise from the dead,

and Christ will shine on you."

15 Be very careful, then, how you live—not as unwise but as wise, 16 making the most of every opportunity, because the days are evil. 17 Therefore do not be foolish, but understand what the Lord's will is. 18 Do not get drunk on wine, which leads to debauchery. Instead, be filled with the Spirit. 19 Speak to one another with psalms, hymns and spiritual songs. Sing and make music in your heart to the Lord, 20 always giving thanks to God the Father for everything, in the name of our Lord Jesus Christ.

21 Submit to one another out of reverence for Christ.

Jesus came that we might have life and have it to the full. That's his life and his life is a light that sets us free form Darkness and gives us a new way of living. For He who the Son sets free is free indeed.

John 8:34–36 (NIV84) 34 Jesus replied, "I tell you the truth, everyone who sins is a slave to sin. 35 Now a slave has no permanent place in the family, but a son belongs to it forever. 36 So if the Son sets you free, you will be free indeed.

Let us start out this New Year with a passion for the Life and Word of Christ living and shining in our hearts that we may know the freedom that belongs to the true Children of God.

HIDING ETERNAL LIFE

This message is keying off the previous message of "Internal Light". In that message I showed how Jesus is that Eternal Life that was with the Father in the beginning. And it is that Life that is the Light to the souls of all who go on believing and receive him into their hearts. Darkness would be bored in heaven because all that is there is Light. Darkness would have nothing to feed upon. We now are going to delve more deeply into that Concept of Eternal Life.

God has always protected eternal life. Before the fall of Adam and Eve the Tree of Life stood open and unprotected in the Garden of Eden. But immediately after the fall of mankind came God's protection of eternal life.

> Genesis 3:21–24 (NIV84) 21 The LORD God made garments of skin for Adam and his wife and clothed them. 22 And the LORD God said, "The man has now become like one of us, knowing good and evil. He must not be allowed to reach out his hand and take also from the tree of life and eat and live forever." 23 So the LORD God banished him from the Garden of Eden to work the ground from which he had been taken. 24 After he drove the man out, he placed on the east side of the Garden of Eden cherubim and a flaming sword flashing back and forth to guard the way to the tree of life.

God does not make eternal life available just to anyone, but it is available to all who will repent and turn to Christ. He is not going to give eternal life to those who are bent on continuing in sin lest sin become eternal. There comes a time when sin will be no more, and God continues to hide and protect Eternal life. As was previously reveal in the last message Jesus is the Eternal life that existed with the Father at the beginning.

> 1 John 1:1–4 (NIV84)   That which was from the beginning, which we have heard, which we have seen with our eyes, which we have looked at and our hands have touched—this we proclaim concerning the Word of life. 2 The life appeared; we have seen it and testify to it, and we proclaim to you the eternal life, which was with the Father and has appeared to us. 3 We proclaim to you what we have seen and heard, so that you also may have fellowship with us. And our fellowship is with the Father and with his Son, Jesus Christ. 4 We write this to make our joy complete.

So now Eternal life is hidden in the Son. Those who come to him in repentance and faith he gives eternal life here and now, in this life. That is why Jesus is the only way to the Father, regardless of what Oprah says. The Spiritual Blind can talk about the facts of Christianity, but they cannot see the truth apart from Christ. There is a veil over their spiritual eyes that is only removed in Christ Jesus. But for all that reach out to Christ and receive him there is a river of living water that leads to Eternal Life. Jesus proclaimed it clearly,

> John 14:6 (NIV84) 6 Jesus answered, "I am the way and the truth and the life. No one comes to the Father except through me.

John 4:13–14 (NIV84) 13 Jesus answered, "Everyone who drinks this water will be thirsty again, 14 but whoever drinks the water I give him will never thirst. Indeed, the water I give him will become in him a spring of water welling up to eternal life."

John 5:24–27 (NIV84) 24 "I tell you the truth, whoever hears my word and believes him who sent me has eternal life and will not be condemned; he has crossed over from death to life. 25 I tell you the truth, a time is coming and has now come when the dead will hear the voice of the Son of God and those who hear will live. 26 For as the Father has life in himself, so he has granted the Son to have life in himself. 27 And he has given him authority to judge because he is the Son of Man.

John 12:25–26 (NIV84) 25 The man who loves his life will lose it, while the man who hates his life in this world will keep it for eternal life. 26 Whoever serves me must follow me; and where I am, my servant also will be. My Father will honor the one who serves me.

Eternal Life is hidden in Christ, and it only comes to life in the hearts of those who truly believe. There are many who say they believe but they are shocked when they find out what Jesus said and taught. There is like a mindless faith out there that believes in this mythical figure who never said anything, and people just attribute their beliefs and attitudes to him.

2 Thessalonians 2:10–12 (NIV84) 10 and in every sort of evil that deceives those who are perishing. They perish because they refused to love the truth and so be saved. 11 For this reason God sends them a powerful delusion so that they will believe the lie 12 and so that all will be condemned who have not believed the truth but have delighted in wickedness.

But true believers are not turned off by the Words of Christ and God's Word, the Scriptures, but instead are instructed, encouraged, corrected and led by them.

Eternal Life is also hidden in heaven. A Tree and River of life exists in the Heavens. Those who overcome through Christ's Life and light will drink from that river and eat from that tree.

Revelation 2:7 (NIV84) 7 He who has an ear, let him hear what the Spirit says to the churches. To him who overcomes, I will give the right to eat from the tree of life, which is in the paradise of God.

Revelation 22:1–5 (NIV84)   Then the angel showed me the river of the water of life, as clear as crystal, flowing from the throne of God and of the Lamb 2 down the middle of the great street of the city. On each side of the river stood the tree of life, bearing twelve crops of fruit, yielding its fruit every month. And the leaves of the tree are for the healing of the nations. 3 No longer will there be any curse. The throne of God and of the Lamb will be in the city, and his servants will serve him. 4 They will see his face, and his name will be on their foreheads. 5 There will be no more night. They will not need the light of a lamp or the light of the sun, for the Lord God will give them light. And they will reign for ever and ever.

Revelation 22:14–15 (NIV84) 14 "Blessed are those who wash their robes, that they may have the right to the tree of life and may go through the gates into the city. 15 Outside are the dogs, those who practice magic arts, the sexually immoral, the murderers, the idolaters and everyone who loves and practices falsehood.

Revelation 22:18–19 (NIV84) 18 I warn everyone who hears the words of the prophecy of this book: If anyone adds anything to them, God will add to him the plagues described in this book. 19 And if anyone takes words away from this book of prophecy, God will take away from him his share in the tree of life and in the holy city, which are described in this book.

Eternal life is found in one of three places: The Garden of Eden, in Jesus Christ, and in Heaven. Only one of these three is accessible to us here and now, Jesus Christ. Jesus said that unless you are born-again you cannot inherit the Kingdom of God. Won't you ask him into your heart now and enjoy the freedom of the Children of God. Pray and ask him into your life and don't stop until you know that Eternal life has entered your life in the person of Jesus Christ. You will be known by others by what your life produces.

HAVING TROUBLE WITH AN EMPTY PURSE?

As we begin, we need to learn some things that most churches leave out of their theology. Most if all recognize that God is sovereign over the affairs of men and that He is the King of kings and Lord of Lords. But what many ignore, and some would never say because they always want to speak "Positive" things, is that God has an Angle called the Destroyer. His name clearly identifies his purpose and activity upon the earth. He is used for many purposes to bring about the plans and purposes of God. Let's look at a few.

- He is the Angel that went through Egypt on Passover Night and killed the firstborn of every household which did not have blood on the Door Post as God prescribed. Exodus 12:23 and Hebrews 11:28.

- Because King David listened to Satanic influences and ordered a Census of Israel God ordered the Destroyer to act against Israel & Jerusalem. First Chronicles 21:1-30.

- The Lord sends the Destroyer against the Moabites. Isaiah 16:4

- The Destroyer is a work to protect the Heritage of the Lord for His Servants:

Isaiah 54:16–17 (NIV84)
16 "See, it is I who created the blacksmith
who fans the coals into flame
and forges a weapon fit for its work.
And it is I who have created the destroyer to work havoc;
17 no weapon forged against you will prevail,
and you will refute every tongue that accuses you.
This is the heritage of the servants of the LORD,
and this is their vindication from me,"
declares the LORD.

- The Destroyer uses a Nation from the North to come against Jerusalem for their sins. Jeremiah 4:7 & 6:26 & 12:12 & 22:7 & 48:8, 15, 18, 32 & 51:48, 56
- Something to consider is that God even sends the Destroyer among his people when they act wickedly and forget to honor him. The Apostle Paul refers to this to the Corinthians in First Corinthians 10:6-13, especially verse 10.
- In Revelations 11:15-19 the Destroying Angel goes to work against those who destroy the Earth at the Seventh Trumpet.

When God's people do not support His work God sends the Destroying angel to hinder theirs, and that brings us to the "Purse with holes in it".

Haggai 1:3–11 (NIV84) 3 Then the word of the LORD came through the prophet Haggai: 4 "Is it a time for you yourselves to be living in your paneled houses, while this house remains a ruin?"

5 Now this is what the LORD Almighty says: "Give careful thought to your ways. 6 You have planted much, but have harvested little. You eat, but never have enough. You drink,

but never have your fill. You put on clothes, but are not warm. You earn wages, only to put them in a purse with holes in it."

7 This is what the LORD Almighty says: "Give careful thought to your ways. 8 Go up into the mountains and bring down timber and build the house, so that I may take pleasure in it and be honored," says the LORD. 9 "You expected much, but see, it turned out to be little. What you brought home, I blew away. Why?" declares the LORD Almighty. "Because of my house, which remains a ruin, while each of you is busy with his own house. 10 Therefore, because of you the heavens have withheld their dew and the earth its crops. 11 I called for a drought on the fields and the mountains, on the grain, the new wine, the oil and whatever the ground produces, on men and cattle, and on the labor of your hands."

The Destroyer is at work with Tithes and Offerings as well. Those who Tithe God rebukes the Destroyer in their behalf and prospers the work of their hands. To those who withhold the tithe the Destroyer is at work in their lives and they wonder why they can't break even.

Malachi 3:6–18 (NIV84) Robbing God

6 "I the LORD do not change. So you, O descendants of Jacob, are not destroyed. 7 Ever since the time of your forefathers you have turned away from my decrees and have not kept them. Return to me, and I will return to you," says the LORD Almighty.

"But you ask, 'How are we to return?'

8 "Will a man rob God? Yet you rob me.

"But you ask, 'How do we rob you?'

"In tithes and offerings. 9 You are under a curse—the whole nation of you—because you are robbing me. 10 Bring the whole tithe into the storehouse, that there may be food in my house. Test me in this," says the LORD Almighty, "and see if

I will not throw open the floodgates of heaven and pour out so much blessing that you will not have room enough for it. 11 I will (Literally "rebuke the Destroyer") prevent pests from devouring your crops, and the vines in your fields will not cast their fruit," says the LORD Almighty. 12 "Then all the nations will call you blessed, for yours will be a delightful land," says the LORD Almighty.

13 "You have said harsh things against me," says the LORD.

"Yet you ask, 'What have we said against you?'

14 "You have said, 'It is futile to serve God. What did we gain by carrying out his requirements and going about like mourners before the LORD Almighty? 15 But now we call the arrogant blessed. Certainly the evildoers prosper, and even those who challenge God escape.' "

16 Then those who feared the LORD talked with each other, and the LORD listened and heard. A scroll of remembrance was written in his presence concerning those who feared the LORD and honored his name.

17 "They will be mine," says the LORD Almighty, "in the day when I make up my treasured possession. I will spare them, just as in compassion a man spares his son who serves him. 18 And you will again see the distinction between the righteous and the wicked, between those who serve God and those who do not.

    I want to give a couple of Testimonies about giving. I've grown up in the Church all my life but didn't come to know the Lord until I was 25. I was sprinkled Methodist, Confirmed Luther, Convicted Baptist and saved, baptized, and filled in the Assemblies of God. Shortly after I received the Lord, I quit my Job because it was interfering with my Bible study and growth in the Lord. I do Upholstery, so I did just enough work to pay the bills, on my schedule, and other than that worked at trying to find out what God wanted to do with my life through His Word. I was about a month old in the Lord when one Saturday night the Lord spoke to my heart and told me to give $100 in Sundays offering. I had never given more than $5 in an offering in my life, so the Lord and I had a little debate. I tried to talk Him down. I said, "How about $25." He said, "Nope! $100." I said, "How about $50." He said, "Nope! $100." I said, "How about $75." He said, "Nope! $100." I struggled with this as I lay on my bed until I fell asleep. I went to Church and put $100 in the offering plate. I remember watching it go down the pew until it disappeared into the ushers' hands. I had little left. The Pastor spoke about tithing that morning, something I had never heard of before, and I couldn't wait to get home and figure out how much I had made that month on my own. You guessed it. It was exactly $1000. God told me to Tithe before I knew what Tithing was, and I've tithed ever since. I even tithed when I was pioneering a church and only making $400 per month. My dad was an accountant, and he couldn't believe I was doing what I was doing and tithing on top of it. But I saw many miracles of God's provision which I don't have time to go into now.

The second testimony concerns the Destroyer. I learned about him early in my Christian experience, so I've had eyes to see him at work. Over the 35 years I've been with the Lord now I have on a couple of occasions forgot to pay my tithes. Each time I saw things breaking down and things going wrong and immediately I've check to see if my tithes are up to date. I immediately corrected the oversight and have seen the blessing return as well as the losses.

There are those who have "Tried" Tithing and said it didn't work. To see it work one thing has to be in place; you have to be living within your budget. If you don't have a budget, make one. If you are overspending tithing doesn't guarantee that you get back everything you spent. If you are living within your budget, you will see less things break down and go wrong when you tithe and vice versa if you don't. If you're living outside your budget and don't tithe it will even be worse.

You might say this is a negative message and I don't like the thought of God having a Destroying Angel. Like it or not he exists and serves the King of kings and Lord of lords. But this is a positive message in that if you recognize that this dynamic is at work and you work a budget and tithe you will see money appear that you didn't think you would have and the Work of the Kingdom of God will increase because you are freeing up those he calls to full time ministry to be supported and be about the Kings business. Tithe to your Church, bring in the full tithe into his house.

RIGHTEOUSNESS, DEEDS & WORKS

There is a sad state of affairs going on in the American Church; we do not recognize the difference between Righteousness, Deeds and Works. As a result, behavior unbecoming someone professing Godliness is common in the Body of Christ. Today, I'm going to look at these three words. Let's begin ...

Righteousness: To claim to know the Lord was a life changing truth to the Apostles. Both Jesus and the Apostle John said that anyone who claimed to know Him and still walked in darkness was one of two things; A liar or didn't live by the truth. I john 1:6 and John 8:12.

> Matthew 5:17–20 (NIV84) 17 "Do not think that I have come to abolish the Law or the Prophets; I have not come to abolish them but to fulfill them. 18 I tell you the truth, until heaven and earth disappear, not the smallest letter, not the least stroke of a pen, will by any means disappear from the Law until everything is accomplished. 19 Anyone who breaks one of the least of these commandments and teaches others to do the same will be called least in the kingdom of heaven, but whoever practices and teaches these commands will be called great in the kingdom of heaven. 20 For I tell you that unless your righteousness surpasses that of the Pharisees and the teachers of the law, you will certainly not enter the kingdom of heaven.

> John 8:12 (NIV84) 12 When Jesus spoke again to the people,

he said, "I am the light of the world. Whoever follows me will never walk in darkness but will have the light of life."

Everywhere there has been a revival there has been the resurgence of a holiness movement, because to know the Lord is to know The Holy and Pure God. Knowing the Lord is much different than believing He exists. There is no salvation apart from the indwelling of the Holy Spirit and he imparts a "hunger and thirst after righteousness." Jesus drew a line in the sand when he said, For I tell you that unless your righteousness surpasses that of the Pharisees and the teachers of the law, you will certainly not enter the kingdom of heaven. You are not saved by works but your salvation will produce a level of holiness that surpasses that of the religious leaders of Jesus day, unless of course, you receive God's Grace in vain.

This is why Jesus said that not everyone who says, 'Lord, Lord' will enter the Kingdom of God. If we don't take seriously the work of the Spirit in our lives, we will miss the High Calling of Jesus Christ.

Deeds: The natural response to the work of the Spirit of God in the believer's life are righteousness and Deeds.

Deeds are different from works in that deeds come out of a relationship with Jesus and works are trying to earn his acceptance. Again, here Jesus told a parable that showed that deeds are expected and can lead to a judgment of exclusion; the Parable of the Talents and The Sheep and Goats in Matthew 25.

Jesus died that we would no longer live for ourselves but for Him.

2 Corinthians 5:14–15 (NIV84)

14 For Christ's love compels us, because we are convinced that one died for all, and therefore all died. 15 And he died for all, that those who live should no longer live for themselves but for him who died for them and was raised again.

You can't program deeds, they come out of a heart for Jesus that stem from appreciation rather than a desire to earn favor.

Works: Works is trying to do something to find favor with God apart from a living relationship with Christ through New Birth and accepting His work on the Cross for you.

> Ephesians 2:8–10 (NIV84) 8 For it is by grace you have been saved, through faith—and this not from yourselves, it is the gift of God— 9 not by works, so that no one can boast. 10 For we are God's workmanship, created in Christ Jesus to do good works, which God prepared in advance for us to do.

To not be under works you have to receive the Gift of the Spirit of God that works in you to do the deeds he has chosen for you to do.

The Misconception: Not saved by works is one of the most misunderstood statements in the Bible. Paul and Peter are the two that speak this in that Paul recognized that God chose him even though he persecuted the Church prior to conversion. Peter denied Christ and Jesus restored him. So recognized that Jesus came into their lives, as unsaved men, despite their works. But both did many great deeds for Christ. Many modern Christian take this to mean they can act unrighteous as believers, and it doesn't matter. They use the "not-by-works" statement to be an excuse for immorality and other deeds of Darkness. Jesus is not an excuse for wickedness but the reason for a changed and holy life. You can't be a Child of Light while walking in Darkness. The two do not mix.

> Ephesians 4:17–5:21 (NIV84) 17 So I tell you this, and insist on it in the Lord, that you must no longer live as the Gentiles do, in the futility of their thinking. 18 They are darkened in their understanding and separated from the life of God because of the ignorance that is in them due to the hardening of their hearts. 19 Having lost all sensitivity, they have given themselves over to sensuality so as to indulge in every kind of impurity, with a continual lust for more.

20 You, however, did not come to know Christ that way. 21 Surely you heard of him and were taught in him in accordance with the truth that is in Jesus. 22 You were taught, with regard to your former way of life, to put off your old self, which is being corrupted by its deceitful desires; 23 to be made new in the attitude of your minds; 24 and to put on the new self, created to be like God in true righteousness and holiness.

25 Therefore each of you must put off falsehood and speak truthfully to his neighbor, for we are all members of one body. 26 "In your anger do not sin": Do not let the sun go down while you are still angry, 27 and do not give the devil a foothold. 28 He who has been stealing must steal no longer, but must work, doing something useful with his own hands, that he may have something to share with those in need.

29 Do not let any unwholesome talk come out of your mouths, but only what is helpful for building others up according to their needs, that it may benefit those who listen. 30 And do not grieve the Holy Spirit of God, with whom you were sealed for the day of redemption. 31 Get rid of all bitterness, rage and anger, brawling and slander, along with every form of malice. 32 Be kind and compassionate to one another, forgiving each other, just as in Christ God forgave you.

5 Be imitators of God, therefore, as dearly loved children 2 and live a life of love, just as Christ loved us and gave himself up for us as a fragrant offering and sacrifice to God.

3 But among you there must not be even a hint of sexual immorality, or of any kind of impurity, or of greed, because these are improper for God's holy people. 4 Nor should there be obscenity, foolish talk, or coarse joking, which are out of place, but rather thanksgiving. 5 For of this you can be sure: No immoral, impure or greedy person—such a man is an idolater—has any inheritance in the kingdom of Christ and of God. 6 Let no one deceive you with empty words, for

because of such things God's wrath comes on those who are disobedient. 7 Therefore do not be partners with them.

8 For you were once darkness, but now you are light in the Lord. Live as children of light 9 (for the fruit of the light consists in all goodness, righteousness, and truth) 10 and find out what pleases the Lord. 11 Have nothing to do with the fruitless deeds of darkness, but rather expose them. 12 For it is shameful even to mention what the disobedient do in secret. 13 But everything exposed by the light becomes visible, 14 for it is light that makes everything visible. This is why it is said:

"Wake up, O sleeper,

rise from the dead,

and Christ will shine on you."

15 Be very careful, then, how you live—not as unwise but as wise, 16 making the most of every opportunity, because the days are evil. 17 Therefore do not be foolish, but understand what the Lord's will is. 18 Do not get drunk on wine, which leads to debauchery. Instead, be filled with the Spirit. 19 Speak to one another with psalms, hymns and spiritual songs. Sing and make music in your heart to the Lord, 20 always giving thanks to God the Father for everything, in the name of our Lord Jesus Christ.

21 Submit to one another out of reverence for Christ.

I did not receive the Spirit of the Lord by good works, but God did wait for me to come to a place of repentance before giving me the grace of his Spirit. Repentance does not mean perfection; it just means a turning in the direction of the Lord. Turn toward righteousness and good deeds and you will be ready for a rich welcome into the Kingdom of God. Blessings.

REPENTANCE, CONFESSION AND JUSTIFICATION

I'm going to look at three words that have the potential of changing a defeated person into a victorious Christian believer. God wants us to live victoriously in this life, not being bogged down with the baggage of this world. Three words will lead us to the Victory that only Christ can give. It takes a man or woman with intestinal fortitude (guts) to take hold of the inner strength needed to see their lives changed. Everything I'm about to say to you take some forceful action on your part in dealing with your own spirit. Proverbs says it well …

> Proverbs 16:32 (NIV84)
> 32   Better a patient man than a warrior,
>   a man who controls his temper than one who takes a city.

Repentance: The word comes from two Greek words pushed together; a common occurrence in Greek. "Metanaeo", Meta is a preposition mean "after", and Naeo means "to Think". Repentance is to have an afterthought. It's a good thing too because most of us are not very good at forethought. It's after we chosen a course that we look back and realize that we've left God out of the plan and must go back and change our direction. Therefore, repentance is defined by some as a turning of your direction, which is true. Christianity is simple; Just turn right and go straight. If we try to come to God without getting Repentance right, we will mess up the following two words; Confession and justification and find ourselves without the overcoming power that comes from Christ.

Confession: Is also a word that is made up of two Greek words, a compound. It is Homologos. In Greek there are two words for "Other": other of the same kind "Homo" or another of a different kind "Hetero". Confession means, "Homo" = same and "logos" = words; thus, confession is speaking the same words that God does about sin. If you are not repentant for the directions and actions of your life you will never confess you sin with the attitude that God is looking for. The Apostle John clearly lays out the benefits of true confession of sin ...

> 1 John 1:8–10 (NIV84) 8 If we claim to be without sin, we deceive ourselves and the truth is not in us. 9 If we confess our sins, he is faithful and just and will forgive us our sins and purify us from all unrighteousness. 10 If we claim we have not sinned, we make him out to be a liar and his word has no place in our lives.

What is interesting about this passage is that it leads right into the topic of false justification. Verse 8 and 10 are both two types of false justification which we will look at in a moment. But verse 9 shows the benefits of Biblical Confession; God will forgive and purify. Purification is a work of the Holy Spirit. He will work in your life to remove those things that are causing the need for confession. The problem is we spend too much time trying to justify our sin rather than repenting and turning so we never get to the confession that will bring the blessings of God. This truth is also clearly revealed in scripture.

> Psalm 32:2–5 (NIV84)
> 2   Blessed is the man
> whose sin the LORD does not count against him

and in whose spirit is no deceit.
3   When I kept silent,
my bones wasted away
through my groaning all day long.
4   For day and night
your hand was heavy upon me;
my strength was sapped
as in the heat of summer. Selah
5   Then I acknowledged my sin to you
and did not cover up my iniquity.
I said, "I will confess
my transgressions to the LORD"—
and you forgave
the guilt of my sin. Selah
and another …
Proverbs 28:13 (NIV84)
13 He who conceals his sins does not prosper,
but whoever confesses and renounces them finds mercy.

Justification: You see, self-justification is not the same thing as being justified by God. In a legal proceeding a man may have justifiably killed another in self-protection, but he can never be called justified unless he admits he did the act. If he says he did not kill him when he did, he is not justified by the law. Faith in Christ requires repentance, confession and then justification by God.

The Greek word translated "Justification" also comes from two words: "Dia" a preposition meaning "through" and "kaiw" meaning "burning". In I John 1:9 we read, 9 If we confess our sins, he is faithful and just and will forgive us our sins and purify us from all unrighteousness." That purifying is the burning out of the dross in our lives and justification is the result. God does call us justified even while he is at work in the cleaning process because

He sees the finished product even when we and others do not. The Apostle Paul spoke of the final judgment in term of walking through the fire.

> 1 Corinthians 3:10–15 (NIV84) 10 By the grace God has given me, I laid a foundation as an expert builder, and someone else is building on it. But each one should be careful how he builds. 11 For no one can lay any foundation other than the one already laid, which is Jesus Christ. 12 If any man builds on this foundation using gold, silver, costly stones, wood, hay or straw, 13 his work will be shown for what it is, because the Day will bring it to light. It will be revealed with fire, and the fire will test the quality of each man's work. 14 If what he has built survives, he will receive his reward. 15 If it is burned up, he will suffer loss; he himself will be saved, but only as one escaping through the flames.

And the Apostle Peter spoke of the trials of this life as the fire that prepares us for the Kingdom of God …

> 1 Peter 1:3–9 (NIV84) 3 Praise be to the God and Father of our Lord Jesus Christ! In his great mercy he has given us new birth into a living hope through the resurrection of Jesus Christ from the dead, 4 and into an inheritance that can never perish, spoil or fade—kept in heaven for you, 5 who through faith are shielded by God's power until the coming of the salvation that is ready to be revealed in the last time. 6 In this you greatly rejoice, though now for a little while you may have had to suffer grief in all kinds of trials. 7 These have come so that your faith—of greater worth than gold, which perishes even though refined by fire—may be proved genuine and may result in praise, glory and honor when Jesus Christ is revealed. 8 Though you have not seen him, you love him; and even though you do not see him now, you believe in him and are filled with an inexpressible and glorious joy, 9 for you are receiving the goal of your faith, the salvation of your

souls.

If you want to be victorious in your Christian walk, I encourage you to turn in repentance, Confess your sin with words that match God's words about it, and reject self-justification in looking to God to do his purifying work in your life. As Jesus said in the Beatitudes, "Blessed is he who hungers and thirsts after righteousness for he shall be filled." Ask him into your life today with a heart that God can honor.
Blessings

WHICH ARE YOU?

Many are opposing Christianity today through their false views of what a Christian Is. TV shows portray them as carnal, self-seeking women who place beauty and position over Godly virtue. Scripture shows people in varying states of spiritual development or deformity. Today I'm going to reveal some of those personas and we can each judge for ourselves and see where we stand.

MOCKERS:

As the USA turns from its Christian roots and Churches refuse to take a stand for the truth, mockers increase. Everyone talks about human rights, but the Kingdom of God is about God's rights. He is building his Kingdom in the hearts of men, women and children, and that Kingdom is based on His Character not on a legislative session. Mockers have always existed, and I don't expect that they will ever disappear until God makes up His Kingdom and destroys this earth. God's wisdom is only revealed in Christ:

> 1 Corinthians 1:18–25 (NIV84) 18 For the message of the cross is foolishness to those who are perishing, but to us who are being saved it is the power of God. 19 For it is written:
>
> "I will destroy the wisdom of the wise;
>
> the intelligence of the intelligent I will frustrate."
>
> 20 Where is the wise man? Where is the scholar? Where is the philosopher of this age? Has not God made foolish the wisdom of the world? 21 For since in the wisdom of God the world through its wisdom did not know him, God was pleased through the foolishness of what was preached to save

those who believe. 22 Jews demand miraculous signs and Greeks look for wisdom, 23 but we preach Christ crucified: a stumbling block to Jews and foolishness to Gentiles, 24 but to those whom God has called, both Jews and Greeks, Christ the power of God and the wisdom of God. 25 For the foolishness of God is wiser than man's wisdom, and the weakness of God is stronger than man's strength.

And Paul continues ...

1 Corinthians 2:6–16 (NIV84) 6 We do, however, speak a message of wisdom among the mature, but not the wisdom of this age or of the rulers of this age, who are coming to nothing. 7 No, we speak of God's secret wisdom, a wisdom that has been hidden and that God destined for our glory before time began. 8 None of the rulers of this age understood it, for if they had, they would not have crucified the Lord of glory. 9 However, as it is written:

"No eye has seen,

no ear has heard,

no mind has conceived,

what God has prepared for those who love him"—

10 but God has revealed it to us by his Spirit.

The Spirit searches all things, even the deep things of God. 11 For who among men knows the thoughts of a man except the man's spirit within him? In the same way no one knows the thoughts of God except the Spirit of God. 12 We have not received the spirit of the world but the Spirit who is from God, that we may understand what God has freely given us. 13 This is what we speak, not in words taught us by human wisdom but in words taught by the Spirit, expressing spiritual truths in spiritual words. 14 The man without the Spirit does not accept the things that come from the Spirit of God, for they are foolishness to him, and he cannot understand them, because they are spiritually discerned. 15

The spiritual man makes judgments about all things, but he himself is not subject to any man's judgment:

16 "For who has known the mind of the Lord that he may instruct him?"

But we have the mind of Christ.

SCOFFERS

Scoffers will come but they speak of what they do not understand and shall eventually fall under the judgment of God's Law.

> 2 Peter 3:3–7 (NIV84) 3 First of all, you must understand that in the last days scoffers will come, scoffing and following their own evil desires. 4 They will say, "Where is this 'coming' he promised? Ever since our fathers died, everything goes on as it has since the beginning of creation." 5 But they deliberately forget that long ago by God's word the heavens existed and the earth was formed out of water and by water. 6 By these waters also the world of that time was deluged and destroyed. 7 By the same word the present heavens and earth are reserved for fire, being kept for the day of judgment and destruction of ungodly men.

EVER LEARNING BUT UNABLE TO COME TO A KNOWDGE OF THE TRUTH:

Just above scoffers are those who have learned many things about Christ and the Kingdom of God, but it never takes enough root in their lives to cause them to act upon it. They profess faith but live like and hold the beliefs and attitudes of the World. The Apostle Paul also addresses them when he wrote to one of his understudies, Timothy.

> 2 Timothy 3:1–9 (NIV84)   But mark this: There will be terrible times in the last days. 2 People will be lovers

of themselves, lovers of money, boastful, proud, abusive, disobedient to their parents, ungrateful, unholy, 3 without love, unforgiving, slanderous, without self-control, brutal, not lovers of the good, 4 treacherous, rash, conceited, lovers of pleasure rather than lovers of God— 5 having a form of godliness but denying its power. Have nothing to do with them.

6 They are the kind who worm their way into homes and gain control over weak-willed women, who are loaded down with sins and are swayed by all kinds of evil desires, 7 always learning but never able to acknowledge the truth. 8 Just as Jannes and Jambres opposed Moses, so also these men oppose the truth—men of depraved minds, who, as far as the faith is concerned, are rejected. 9 But they will not get very far because, as in the case of those men, their folly will be clear to everyone.

Today there are whole churches that fall into this group. They hold to rituals and forms but have not come to a transforming knowledge of Jesus Christ. They cry out "once saved, always saved" as an excuse to live an ungodly life and skirt the issues of walking with Christ.

THEIR GOD IS THEIR STOMACH:

Another stance is those who proclaim faith in Christ but it is all about them. God is just a means of acquiring things and status. God does bless those who serve him, but they will also experience the struggles associated with taking a stand against the world. But these focus on acquiring rather than serving and they broke the Apostle Paul's heart as he wrote about them.

Philippians 3:17–21 (NIV84) 17 Join with others in following my example, brothers, and take note of those who live according to the pattern we gave you. 18 For, as I have often told you before and now say again even with tears, many live as enemies of the cross of Christ. 19 Their destiny is destruction, their god is their stomach, and their glory is in their shame. Their mind is on earthly things. 20 But our citizenship is in heaven. And we eagerly await a Savior from there, the Lord Jesus Christ, 21 who, by the power that enables him to bring everything under his control, will transform our lowly bodies so that they will be like his glorious body.

Jesus came to serve, and he washed His disciples feet to teach them the proper attitude about their stay here on this earth.

THE UNREPENTENT BELIEVER:

This includes the simple, the mocker, the fool and those who have known the Lord and have walked with him until they come to a place where they don't want to listen to His direction in their lives. God would have made his thoughts known to them if they would repent but in their stubbornness, they lose the blessings of God. God the Father speaking in Proverbs 1 speaks to this.

Proverbs 1:22–33 (NIV84)

22 "How long will you simple ones love your simple ways?

How long will mockers delight in mockery

and fools hate knowledge?

23 If you had responded to my rebuke,

I would have poured out my heart to you

and made my thoughts known to you.

24 But since you rejected me when I called

and no one gave heed when I stretched out my hand,

25 since you ignored all my advice

and would not accept my rebuke,

26 I in turn will laugh at your disaster;

I will mock when calamity overtakes you—
27   when calamity overtakes you like a storm,
when disaster sweeps over you like a whirlwind,
when distress and trouble overwhelm you.
28   "Then they will call to me but I will not answer;
they will look for me but will not find me.
29   Since they hated knowledge
and did not choose to fear the LORD,
30   since they would not accept my advice
and spurned my rebuke,
31   they will eat the fruit of their ways
and be filled with the fruit of their schemes.
32   For the waywardness of the simple will kill them,
and the complacency of fools will destroy them;
33   but whoever listens to me will live in safety
and be at ease, without fear of harm."

Those who live in the Kingdom of God will have spent their lives choosing God's ways. Jesus asked the religious of His day, "why do you call me Lord, Lord and don't do what I say?" God is long suffering, but the witness his people leave in the light of their disobedience affects those around them.

SEEKING THE LORD WITH ALL OF THEIR HEART:

There are those who seek God with all their heart. As it's said in Jeremiah 29:13 (NIV84) 13 You will seek me and find me when you seek me with all your heart. This is why Jesus said, "hard is the way and few there be that find it."

Those who continually seek the Lord will find their lives and thinking changed as is written in Proverbs chapter 2.

Proverbs 2:1–11 (NIV84)

> 2   My son, if you accept my words
> and store up my commands within you,
> 2   turning your ear to wisdom
> and applying your heart to understanding,
> 3   and if you call out for insight
> and cry aloud for understanding,
> 4   and if you look for it as for silver
> and search for it as for hidden treasure,
> 5   then you will understand the fear of the LORD
> and find the knowledge of God.
> 6   For the LORD gives wisdom,
> and from his mouth come knowledge and understanding.
> 7   He holds victory in store for the upright,
> he is a shield to those whose walk is blameless,
> 8   for he guards the course of the just
> and protects the way of his faithful ones.
> 9   Then you will understand what is right and just
> and fair—every good path.
> 10   For wisdom will enter your heart,
> and knowledge will be pleasant to your soul.
> 11   Discretion will protect you,
> and understanding will guard you.

Friends and family of those who are seekers will see the changed lives of those who seek the Lord. Jesus said, "Blessed are those who hunger and thirst after righteousness." It is a life changing thing to lay hold of the Son of God.

PRESSING TOWARD THE GOAL:

That seeking is transformed into a pressing toward a mark that is higher than they can reach. But their love for the Father, the

Son and the Holy Spirit compels them to act and live in such a way that God is pleased. Paul again speaks of that internal drive to live for God.

> Philippians 3:7-16 (NIV84) 7 But whatever was to my profit I now consider loss for the sake of Christ. 8 What is more, I consider everything a loss compared to the surpassing greatness of knowing Christ Jesus my Lord, for whose sake I have lost all things. I consider them rubbish, that I may gain Christ 9 and be found in him, not having a righteousness of my own that comes from the law, but that which is through faith in Christ—the righteousness that comes from God and is by faith. 10 I want to know Christ and the power of his resurrection and the fellowship of sharing in his sufferings, becoming like him in his death, 11 and so, somehow, to attain to the resurrection from the dead.
>
> 12 Not that I have already obtained all this, or have already been made perfect, but I press on to take hold of that for which Christ Jesus took hold of me. 13 Brothers, I do not consider myself yet to have taken hold of it. But one thing I do: Forgetting what is behind and straining toward what is ahead, 14 I press on toward the goal to win the prize for which God has called me heavenward in Christ Jesus.
>
> 15 All of us who are mature should take such a view of things. And if on some point you think differently, that too God will make clear to you. 16 Only let us live up to what we have already attained.

OVERCOMERS:

The Christians' goal is to become an Overcomer. Not accepting the values, desires, philosophies, and desires of the people of this world, but instead are readying themselves for citizenship in the Kingdom of God.

> 2 Corinthians 5:13-15 (NIV84) 13 If we are out of our mind,

it is for the sake of God; if we are in our right mind, it is for you. 14 For Christ's love compels us, because we are convinced that one died for all, and therefore all died. 15 And he died for all, that those who live should no longer live for themselves but for him who died for them and was raised again.

Jesus died that we our separation from God would be destroyed and through being indwelt by God's Spirit our lives would be changed to the point that we no longer live for ourselves but for He who loved us so much as to give himself for us.

1 John 4:4–6 (NIV84) 4 You, dear children, are from God and have overcome them, because the one who is in you is greater than the one who is in the world. 5 They are from the world and therefore speak from the viewpoint of the world, and the world listens to them. 6 We are from God, and whoever knows God listens to us; but whoever is not from God does not listen to us. This is how we recognize the Spirit of truth and the spirit of falsehood.

This passage has been used by many groups to justify teaching that counter's God's Word. Those you need to listen to are words of the Jesus Christ and the Apostles. The test that one is following Christ is that His words and those of His Apostles become extremely important in their lives.

The final test is in which of these scenarios best represents you? Are you walking in the Way or playing in the World. Jesus said that not everyone that says, "Lord, Lord" will enter the Kingdom of God. Are you living the life or just looking for fire insurance?

2 Corinthians 13:5–6 (NIV84) 5 Examine yourselves to see whether you are in the faith; test yourselves. Do you not realize that Christ Jesus is in you—unless, of course, you fail the test? 6 And I trust that you will discover that we have not

failed the test.

I pray that you will pass God's Test when we all will stand before the Judgment seat of God, and it will not be by the laws of men that He will be judging.

ONLY YOU CAN PREVENT WILDFIRES

When wildfires break out the fire department will go to the site and establish a perimeter and do a controlled burn around it to cause it to burn out. Misconceptions about spirituality fire abound and only the Holy Scriptures, the Bible, provides the touchstone by which we can test the spirit. The Apostle John warned us:

> 1 John 4:1 (NIV84) Dear friends, do not believe every spirit, but test the spirits to see whether they are from God, because many false prophets have gone out into the world.

John goes on to deal with the error of his day and that was those who said Jesus came in a spiritual body and not in the flesh. But Jesus himself said they would come in sheep's clothing, and you could only know them by their fruit. Jesus never said you would know his people by their confession of faith alone, but that you would know them by their fruit.

One of the characteristics of a child is that everything goes into their mouth. They take everything in. So those who are mature need to produce a protective environment in which they are safe. We all need to be discerning and discernment only comes through the Word of God.

I'm going to look at some misconceptions about Spirituality taken from God's Word that will act as a safeguard against "Wildfire" that destroys the forests of God rather than helping them to grow.

- The Spirit comes upon me:

There are those who make twitches and sounds like the Holy Spirit is coming upon them. The twitches and sounds have no Biblical basis. But even more important is that the concept of the Spirit coming upon a person is an Old Testament concept. The teaching of the New Testament is that the Holy Spirit lives within the converted believer and is in constant communication with the Born-Again. The Holy Spirit is the "Parakalete". Para is a Greek preposition meaning "alongside", and Kaleo means "called", thus the Holy Spirit is called alongside the converted and is with them constantly.

- The Spirit is different than Jesus:

There are those who say the Holy Spirit is different than Jesus and so brings new things into the believer's life that Jesus never did. There are to Greek words for Another. Homo; another of the same kind, and Hetero; another of a different kind. When Jesus told his disciple that he would send them the Holy Spirit he said he would send them "Another of the same kind" as himself. The Holy Spirit doesn't act differently than Jesus did because the Spirit of Christ is the same as the Holy Spirit.

> John 14:15–21 (NIV84) 15 "If you love me, you will obey what I command. 16 And I will ask the Father, and he will give you another Counselor to be with you forever— 17 the Spirit of truth. The world cannot accept him, because it neither sees him nor knows him. But you know him, for he lives with you and will be in you. 18 I will not leave you as orphans; I will come to you. 19 Before long, the world will not see me anymore, but you will see me. Because I live, you also will live. 20 On that day you will realize that I am in my Father, and you are in me, and I am in you. 21 Whoever has my commands and obeys them, he is the one who loves me. He

who loves me will be loved by my Father, and I too will love him and show myself to him."

The Father, the Son and the Holy Spirit are three in one. Jesus told his disciples that he who had seen him had seen the Father as well. Strange Fire is a fire that comes from a different place.

- Quakers and Shakers

Shortly after the founding of our country two groups of people came over from England. The Quakers and the Shakers. They personified the concept of the Holy Spirit coming upon you and exhibiting strange twitches, shakings, and sounds. Some of them would fall in the street in the middle of the town and lay there for hours. This has affected some Pentecostal and Charismatic circles ever since. They had "modern day prophets" some of which they held higher than Jesus. After 30 years of Pentecostal Ministry, I've never experienced any Quaking and Shaking, but I've been awakened from sleep on numerous occasions as the Lord has spoken to my heart as well has bring the Word of God to my heart in times of need. I love his Spirit and the Work of the Spirit in my life, but I have tested the Spirit of the Super Spiritual over the past 30 years and have found problems with the heart which I will discuss shortly. But first the Super Spiritual.

- A Super Spirituality that Neglects the Issues of the Heart:

A great danger to those who would be involved in powers is that they become focused on God doing thing in the external that they neglect the internal.

Proverbs 4:23-27 (NIV84)

23   Above all else, guard your heart,
for it is the wellspring of life.

24   Put away perversity from your mouth;

keep corrupt talk far from your lips.

25   Let your eyes look straight ahead,

fix your gaze directly before you.

26   Make level paths for your feet

and take only ways that are firm.

27   Do not swerve to the right or the left;

keep your foot from evil.

God is a spiritual fruit grower and when people remove their focus from internal fruit to outward demonstrations they can move into "Wild, Strange, unauthorized Fire" that is not acceptable to God as an offering before Him.

Leviticus 10:1–3 (NIV84) The Death of Nadab and Abihu

10   Aaron's sons Nadab and Abihu took their censers, put fire in them and added incense; and they offered unauthorized fire before the LORD, contrary to his command. 2 So fire came out from the presence of the LORD and consumed them, and they died before the LORD. 3 Moses then said to Aaron, "This is what the LORD spoke of when he said:

" 'Among those who approach me

I will show myself holy;

in the sight of all the people

I will be honored.' "

Aaron remained silent.

You can become more interested in playing with power than in maintaining a pure and clean heart. Many have fallen because they have neglected the heart. There will be many who claim great things who will find that they neglected the most important thing, their heart.

Matthew 7:21–23 (NIV84) 21 "Not everyone who says to me, 'Lord, Lord,' will enter the kingdom of heaven, but only he who does the will of my Father who is in heaven. 22 Many will say to me on that day, 'Lord, Lord, did we not prophesy in your name, and in your name drive out demons and perform many miracles?' 23 Then I will tell them plainly, 'I never knew you. Away from me, you evildoers!'

I want Jesus to say, "Well done good and faithful servant" when I stand before Him; not, "Be gone you worker of iniquity!" I want to be used by God in every way he sees fit, but I'm not going to stop keeping a watch upon my heart.

- Loosing Connection with the Head:

There are groups that have come to so focus on the prophetic that their services totally consist of the telling of Visions and Dreams and have left the Word of God completely, which is the true sword of the Spirit.

Colossians 2:18–19 (NIV84) 18 Do not let anyone who delights in false humility and the worship of angels disqualify you for the prize. Such a person goes into great detail about what he has seen, and his unspiritual mind puffs him up with idle notions. 19 He has lost connection with the Head, from whom the whole body, supported and held together by its ligaments and sinews, grows as God causes it to grow.

The Word of God is what the Spirit uses, and it is what the Spirit uses to cause a burning in the hearts and souls and bones of men and women and children.

Hebrews 4:12–13 (NIV84) 12 For the word of God is living and active. Sharper than any double-edged sword, it penetrates even to dividing soul and spirit, joints and marrow; it judges the thoughts and attitudes of the heart. 13 Nothing in all creation is hidden from God's sight. Everything is uncovered and laid bare before the eyes of him to whom we must give account.

Watch out for the super-spiritual who would move you away from God's Word. But test everything by the Word of God.

- The Coming of False Prophets:

Jesus said in the last days there would come many claiming to be prophets and saviors. Concerning all his people he didn't say that you would know them by their confession of faith but by their fruit. Those who have been born of his Spirit and watch their heart will live an act in line with his Word for they will hunger and thirst after God's righteousness. Jesus words make it clear.

Matthew 7:15–23 (NIV84) 15 "Watch out for false prophets. They come to you in sheep's clothing, but inwardly they are ferocious wolves. 16 By their fruit you will recognize them. Do people pick grapes from thornbushes, or figs from thistles? 17 Likewise every good tree bears good fruit, but a bad tree bears bad fruit. 18 A good tree cannot bear bad fruit, and a bad tree cannot bear good fruit. 19 Every tree that does not bear good fruit is cut down and thrown into the fire. 20 Thus, by their fruit you will recognize them.

21 "Not everyone who says to me, 'Lord, Lord,' will enter the kingdom of heaven, but only he who does the will of my Father who is in heaven. 22 Many will say to me on that day, 'Lord, Lord, did we not prophesy in your name, and in your name drive out demons and perform many miracles?' 23 Then I will tell them plainly, 'I never knew you. Away from me, you evildoers!'

There needs to be those in the church today who are spiritually sensitive and have an authorized fire in their heart and bones that is sent from God. But there are counterfeits also. Test the Spirit's to see if they are from God, but you can only do that if you yourself are true and have the Word of God burning in your heart. Don't just assume that your ways are God's ways, test your ways by the Word of God. It's the only thing I am sure of. It is my rock, and it has led me to the Rock that is a true foundation.

- Conclusions: Maintaining a Controlled Burn!

Seeking the Lord with all your heart and desire his fire to burn in your heart to speak the Word of God. The Sword of the Spirit is the Written Word, so put it in your heart so that out of the abundance of the heart the mouth will seek. Outward gyrations do not have the same power or source as the Word of God spoken from a fire within.

Jeremiah 20:7–10 (NIV84) Jeremiah's Complaint

7   O LORD, you deceived me, and I was deceived;
you overpowered me and prevailed.
I am ridiculed all day long;
everyone mocks me.
8   Whenever I speak, I cry out
proclaiming violence and destruction.
So the word of the LORD has brought me
insult and reproach all day long.
9   But if I say, "I will not mention him
or speak any more in his name,"
his word is in my heart like a fire,
a fire shut up in my bones.
I am weary of holding it in;
indeed, I cannot.
10   I hear many whispering,
"Terror on every side!
Report him! Let's report him!"
All my friends

are waiting for me to slip, saying,
"Perhaps he will be deceived;
then we will prevail over him
and take our revenge on him."

Don't put out the Spirit's fire, but test everything and hold on to what is good.

1 Thessalonians 5:16–24 (NIV84) 16 Be joyful always; 17 pray continually; 18 give thanks in all circumstances, for this is God's will for you in Christ Jesus.

19 Do not put out the Spirit's fire; 20 do not treat prophecies with contempt. 21 Test everything. Hold on to the good. 22 Avoid every kind of evil.

23 May God himself, the God of peace, sanctify you through and through. May your whole spirit, soul and body be kept blameless at the coming of our Lord Jesus Christ. 24 The one who calls you is faithful and he will do it.

People put down Christians who are excited about the Lord and love to worship him, but they can go to a sporting event or a concert and scream like banshees with painted faces and that's not a problem. I would rather dance with David than stand on the sidelines with Judas. Love the Lord with all your heart, and guard your heart above all things because all the outward expressions in the world will not replace a pure heart on the Day of Lord!

WHAT BASE ARE YOU ON?

Introduction:

Many people believe, but their lives are governed by what they base their faith on. That base colors and defines how they live their lives and eventually will affect how they stand in the Judgment where we will give account to God. So, let's look at some bases and the pros and cons they present.

Definition of Terms:

One word that affects our understanding of our bases the most is the word "Grace". It has been defined as unmerited favor, which is a better definition of mercy than grace. Many define it by what they want it to be rather than going to the source of God's word to define it. It comes from the Greek root "Karis" meaning gift. Again, many just see it as a stagnant gift like one you sit on the shelf and look at. But God's word show that Grace is an active gift, one that needs to be used and maintained. The following passage refers to the Holy Spirit as the Spirit of Grace.

> Hebrews 10:26–31 (NIV84) 26 If we deliberately keep on sinning after we have received the knowledge of the truth, no sacrifice for sins is left, 27 but only a fearful expectation of judgment and of raging fire that will consume the enemies of God. 28 Anyone who rejected the law of Moses died without mercy on the testimony of two or three witnesses. 29 How much more severely do you think a man deserves to be

punished who has trampled the Son of God under foot, who has treated as an unholy thing the blood of the covenant that sanctified him, and who has insulted the Spirit of grace? 30 For we know him who said, "It is mine to avenge; I will repay," and again, "The Lord will judge his people." 31 It is a dreadful thing to fall into the hands of the living God.

The Holy Spirit is an active participant in the Believers life and therefore they are experiencing God's Grace. Here are some clear examples of what the Spirit of God does in His acts of Grace.

Galatians 5:16–26 (NIV84) 16 So I say, live by the Spirit, and you will not gratify the desires of the sinful nature. 17 For the sinful nature desires what is contrary to the Spirit, and the Spirit what is contrary to the sinful nature. They are in conflict with each other, so that you do not do what you want. 18 But if you are led by the Spirit, you are not under law.

19 The acts of the sinful nature are obvious: sexual immorality, impurity and debauchery; 20 idolatry and witchcraft; hatred, discord, jealousy, fits of rage, selfish ambition, dissensions, factions 21 and envy; drunkenness, orgies, and the like. I warn you, as I did before, that those who live like this will not inherit the kingdom of God.

22 But the fruit of the Spirit is love, joy, peace, patience, kindness, goodness, faithfulness, 23 gentleness and self-control. Against such things there is no law. 24 Those who belong to Christ Jesus have crucified the sinful nature with its passions and desires. 25 Since we live by the Spirit, let us keep in step with the Spirit. 26 Let us not become conceited, provoking and envying each other.

Titus 2:11–14 (NIV84) 11 For the grace of God that brings salvation has appeared to all men. 12 It teaches us to say "No" to ungodliness and worldly passions, and to live self-controlled, upright and godly lives in this present age, 13 while we wait for the blessed hope—the glorious appearing of our great God and Savior, Jesus Christ, 14 who gave himself for us to redeem us from all wickedness and to purify for himself a people that are his very own, eager to do what is good.

It is obvious from these passages that God's Grace does not excuse sin in our lives but works to eradicate it. Jesus is not an excuse for wicked behavior but the reason for a converted and transformed life in Christ. The Gift of God is free, but it is not cheap to run and maintain. Now let's look at some bases.

Faith Based Salvation:

Faith based salvation commonly uses the statement that we are not saved by works but by grace (meaning a stagnant gift). And they eventually go to "Saved by Faith Alone", meaning it doesn't matter how I live or act. But they often forget the following verse.

Ephesians 2:8-10 (NIV84) 8 For it is by grace you have been saved, through faith—and this not from yourselves, it is the gift of God— 9 not by works, so that no one can boast. 10 For we are God's workmanship, created in Christ Jesus to do good works, which God prepared in advance for us to do.

God's grace is active, and we are even told in God's Word to spur one another on to love and good works. (Hebrews 10:24) The Apostle James promotes the message that Faith without works is dead.

James 2:14 (NIV84) 14 What good is it, my brothers, if a man claims to have faith but has no deeds? Can such faith save him?

Jesus made many statements saying that there would be people with faith that will not stand in the judgment. The first, not everyone who says Lord, Lord will enter the Kingdom of God.

> Matthew 7:21–23 (NIV84) 21 "Not everyone who says to me, 'Lord, Lord,' will enter the kingdom of heaven, but only he who does the will of my Father who is in heaven. 22 Many will say to me on that day, 'Lord, Lord, did we not prophesy in your name, and in your name drive out demons and perform many miracles?' 23 Then I will tell them plainly, 'I never knew you. Away from me, you evildoers!'

Secondly, there will be those who neglect the Grace of God:

Hebrews 2:1–4 (NIV84) 2 We must pay more careful attention, therefore, to what we have heard, so that we do not drift away. 2 For if the message spoken by angels was binding, and every violation and disobedience received its just punishment, 3 how shall we escape if we ignore such a great salvation? This salvation, which was first announced by the Lord, was confirmed to us by those who heard him. 4 God also testified to it by signs, wonders and various miracles, and gifts of the Holy Spirit distributed according to his will.

Matthew 24:45–51 (NIV84) 45 "Who then is the faithful and wise servant, whom the master has put in charge of the servants in his household to give them their food at the proper time? 46 It will be good for that servant whose master finds him doing so when he returns. 47 I tell you the truth, he will put him in charge of all his possessions. 48 But suppose that servant is wicked and says to himself, 'My master is staying away a long time,' 49 and he then begins to beat his fellow servants and to eat and drink with drunkards. 50 The master of that servant will come on a day when he does not expect him and at an hour he is not aware of. 51 He will cut him to pieces and assign him a place with the hypocrites, where there will be weeping and gnashing of teeth. (also in

Luke 12:42-48)

Hebrews 10:26-27 (NIV84) 26 If we deliberately keep on sinning after we have received the knowledge of the truth, no sacrifice for sins is left, 27 but only a fearful expectation of judgment and of raging fire that will consume the enemies of God.

Thirdly there are those who put to death the work of the Spirit in their lives and the scriptures call them twice dead. Spiritual dead before New Birth and then dead again after they quench the Spirit of God in their lives.

John 15:5-6 (NIV84) 5 "I am the vine; you are the branches. If a man remains in me and I in him, he will bear much fruit; apart from me you can do nothing. 6 If anyone does not remain in me, he is like a branch that is thrown away and withers; such branches are picked up, thrown into the fire and burned.

Hebrews 10:26-31 (NIV84) 26 If we deliberately keep on sinning after we have received the knowledge of the truth, no sacrifice for sins is left, 27 but only a fearful expectation of judgment and of raging fire that will consume the enemies of God. 28 Anyone who rejected the law of Moses died without mercy on the testimony of two or three witnesses. 29 How much more severely do you think a man deserves to be punished who has trampled the Son of God under foot, who has treated as an unholy thing the blood of the covenant that sanctified him, and who has insulted the Spirit of grace? 30 For we know him who said, "It is mine to avenge; I will repay," and again, "The Lord will judge his people." 31 It is a dreadful thing to fall into the hands of the living God.

Jude 12-13 (NIV84) 12 These men are blemishes at your

love feasts, eating with you without the slightest qualm —shepherds who feed only themselves. They are clouds without rain, blown along by the wind; autumn trees, without fruit and uprooted—twice dead. 13 They are wild waves of the sea, foaming up their shame; wandering stars, for whom blackest darkness has been reserved forever.

Jesus said you will recognize them by their fruit.

Matthew 7:16-20 (NIV84) 16 By their fruit you will recognize them. Do people pick grapes from thornbushes, or figs from thistles? 17 Likewise every good tree bears good fruit, but a bad tree bears bad fruit. 18 A good tree cannot bear bad fruit, and a bad tree cannot bear good fruit. 19 Every tree that does not bear good fruit is cut down and thrown into the fire. 20 Thus, by their fruit you will recognize them.

Faith alone is not going to save you. The Godhead are fruit Growers. Read John 15:15-17. And God expects to reap a harvest, as any good fruit grower does.

Another definition problem is Works verses Deed. The same Greek word is used but they come from a completely different heart. A work is doing something to be accepted while a deed is something that comes out of a transformed heart.

Faith only based salivation sees all things as works so figure that it doesn't matter how they live. But God expects to see deeds coming from the Love of God and Man.

Works Based Salvation:

This leads us to Works Based Salvation. Those who are works based are out there trying to do good things to be accepted. But only deeds can come out of a converted and transformed heart. The Apostle John speaks of this converted transformed heart that acts not from obligation but from love.

1 John 5:3–4 (NIV84) 3 This is love for God: to obey his commands. And his commands are not burdensome, 4 for everyone born of God overcomes the world. This is the victory that has overcome the world, even our faith.

The biggest problem with the works-based salvation is that people think that if they have mental agreement with a Churches doctrine, wear a cross and do Good works they are OK. Jesus said very plainly that unless you are Born-Again you will not enter the Kingdom of God, and that is a free gift, it's not earned or deserved. Everyone who is born of the Spirit will lay their crowns down at the feet of Jesus for all the good things they have done because they recognize that apart from Him they would not have done any of them and anything not done through Christ is filthy self-righteousness.

Light Based Salvation:

By my perspective this is the best and firmest Base in Christ. Your faith, your deeds, and your spiritual life are checked by the light test.

John 12:44–46 (NIV84) 44 Then Jesus cried out, "When a man believes in me, he does not believe in me only, but in the one who sent me. 45 When he looks at me, he sees the one who sent me. 46 I have come into the world as a light, so that no one who believes in me should stay in darkness.

If we are walking in God's light we are safe in Christ. Jesus came as a light so that his followers in this life would not walk in darkness.

John 8:12 (NIV84) 12 When Jesus spoke again to the people, he said, "I am the light of the world. Whoever follows me will never walk in darkness, but will have the light of life."

Jesus' goal is that we would become sons and daughters of light, not excusing the darkness.

> John 12:35–36 (NIV84) 35 Then Jesus told them, "You are going to have the light just a little while longer. Walk while you have the light, before darkness overtakes you. The man who walks in the dark does not know where he is going. 36 Put your trust in the light while you have it, so that you may become sons of light." ....

If we claim to know the Lord and walk in darkness the Apostle John left only two Options: One, we are a liar **and/or** do not know the Lord or two, we are a hypocrite, not living by the truth. (The highlighted Greek word translated "and" can also mean "or".)

> 1 John 1:5–10 (NIV84) 5 This is the message we have heard from him and declare to you: God is light; in him there is no darkness at all. 6 If we claim to have fellowship with him yet walk in the darkness, we lie and/or do not live by the truth. 7 But if we walk in the light, as he is in the light, we have fellowship with one another, and the blood of Jesus, his Son, purifies us from all sin.
>
> 8 If we claim to be without sin, we deceive ourselves and the truth is not in us. 9 If we confess our sins, he is faithful and just and will forgive us our sins and purify us from all unrighteousness. 10 If we claim we have not sinned, we make him out to be a liar and his word has no place in our lives.

So, what is walking in darkness mean? We all fall short in many ways, but there are the deeds of darkness that we are required to repent from. Deeds of Darkness are totally unacceptable in the life of a true believer.

Romans 13:11–14 (NIV84) 11 And do this, understanding the present time. The hour has come for you to wake up from your slumber, because our salvation is nearer now than when we first believed. 12 The night is nearly over; the day is almost here. So let us put aside the deeds of darkness and put on the armor of light. 13 Let us behave decently, as in the daytime, not in orgies and drunkenness, not in sexual immorality and debauchery, not in dissension and jealousy. 14 Rather, clothe yourselves with the Lord Jesus Christ, and do not think about how to gratify the desires of the sinful nature.

Ephesians 5:3–14 (NIV84) 3 But among you there must not be even a hint of sexual immorality, or of any kind of impurity, or of greed, because these are improper for God's holy people. 4 Nor should there be obscenity, foolish talk or coarse joking, which are out of place, but rather thanksgiving. 5 For of this you can be sure: No immoral, impure or greedy person—such a man is an idolater—has any inheritance in the kingdom of Christ and of God. 6 Let no one deceive you with empty words, for because of such things God's wrath comes on those who are disobedient. 7 Therefore do not be partners with them.

8 For you were once darkness, but now you are light in the Lord. Live as children of light 9 (for the fruit of the light consists in all goodness, righteousness and truth) 10 and find out what pleases the Lord. 11 Have nothing to do with the fruitless deeds of darkness, but rather expose them. 12 For it is shameful even to mention what the disobedient do in secret. 13 But everything exposed by the light becomes visible, 14 for it is light that makes everything visible. This is why it is said:

"Wake up, O sleeper,

rise from the dead,

and Christ will shine on you."

These sins always influence a person's life. Walking in Darkness leads to spiritual blindness. You think you are OK, but the enemy has blinded you to the light and you confess faith in Christ while you are blind to your captivity to the enemy.

The worst thing about excusing Deeds of Darkness in our lives is that we are really proclaiming, loud and clear, what we really love. If we love the light, we want to live in it. If we love the darkness we want to live in it. Here is the verdict.

> John 3:19–21 (NIV84) 19 This is the verdict: Light has come into the world, but men loved darkness instead of light because their deeds were evil. 20 Everyone who does evil hates the light, and will not come into the light for fear that his deeds will be exposed. 21 But whoever lives by the truth comes into the light, so that it may be seen plainly that what he has done has been done through God."

The Light Test is the best base for salvation because those who walk in the light are the sons and daughters of God.

> 2 Corinthians 5:15 (NIV84) 15 And he died for all, that those who live should no longer live for themselves but for him who died for them and was raised again.

I'll conclude with the words of the Apostle Peter.

> 1 Peter 4:17–18 (NIV84) 17 For it is time for judgment to begin with the family of God; and if it begins with us, what will the outcome be for those who do not obey the gospel of God? 18 And,
> "If it is hard for the righteous to be saved,
> what will become of the ungodly and the sinner?"

Live your lives to be prepared for that day. Be BASED in LIGHT not

STEPHENMANDEVILLE

Darkness.

ENCOURAGEMENT FROM THE GREEK NT – PART IV

There has been much debate over Romans Chapter 7 & 8. Many use Chapter 7 as an excuse saying that the Paul understood the frustration in loving the things of God but not being able to live them out; therefore Paul meant that we are saved by Grace not works as a static gift that we can do nothing about.

First let's look at a little history of the Apostle Paul's life. Paul was trained in legalistic Judaism as a Pharisee, the more conservative of the Jewish sects, from a very early age. He probably didn't ever remember a day without faith in God the Father. The Law is based on human effort, and Paul loved the ways and Character of God; something that is necessary for anyone to truly live a life for God. But he experienced a major problem. He loved the ways and things of God but found himself continually falling short of being able to live them out. This is what chapter 7 is all about; Paul's frustration in living out his faith. He even went to the extreme of persecuting the Church to try to earn God's favor, until Jesus confronted him on the Damascus Road.

Many a Christian have used this passage to show the inability to walk with God and succeed at it. But there is a little hidden Greek treasure in the middle of the last verse of chapter 7, verse 25, that clears it all up.

> Thanks be to God—through Jesus Christ our Lord! So then, I myself in my mind am a slave to God's law, but in the sinful nature a slave to the law of sin.

Black, M., Martini, C. M., Metzger, B. M., & Wikgren, A. (1997). *The Greek New Testament* (Ro 7:25). Federal Republic of Germany: United Bible Societies.

It looks like APA, but the P is actually an R sound. ARA. is a untranslatable Greek Treasure. It denotes a frustration with the past as a change is made from the former to the later. Chapter 7 is about Paul's life prior to Salvation and Chapter 8 the change and freedom he found in Christ. Pay attention to Paul's words in the intro to Chapter 8.

> Romans 8:1–4 (NIV84) 8 **Therefore**, there is now no condemnation for those who are in Christ Jesus, 2 because through Christ Jesus the law of the Spirit of life set me free from the law of sin and death. 3 For what the law was powerless to do in that it was weakened by the sinful nature, God did by sending his own Son in the likeness of sinful man to be a sin offering. And so, he condemned sin in sinful man, 4 in order that the righteous requirements of the law might be fully met in us, who do not live according to the sinful nature but according to the Spirit.

Paul found a way to obey and walk with God and it was through the Spirit of God and of Jesus Christ. Those without the Holy Spirit cannot obey God, but those with the Spirit have a choice. They can follow the Spirit of the Lord and be saved or follow their flesh and be condemned. That is what verses 5-11 of Romans 8 talks about.

> Romans 8:5–11 (NIV84) 5 Those who live according to the sinful nature have their minds set on what that nature desires; but those who live in accordance with the Spirit have their minds set on what the Spirit desires. 6 The mind of sinful man is death, but the mind controlled by the Spirit is

life and peace; 7 the sinful mind is hostile to God. It does not submit to God's law, nor can it do so. 8 Those controlled by the sinful nature cannot please God.

9 You, however, are controlled not by the sinful nature but by the Spirit, if the Spirit of God lives in you. And if anyone does not have the Spirit of Christ, he does not belong to Christ. 10 But if Christ is in you, your body is dead because of sin, yet your spirit is alive because of righteousness. 11 And if the Spirit of him who raised Jesus from the dead is living in you, he who raised Christ from the dead will also give life to your mortal bodies through his Spirit, who lives in you.

Born again Christians sin by choice, not out of bondage to sin. We who have received the Spirit of the Lord have an obligation, as the Apostle tells us, to walk according to the Spirit. Our very salvation depends upon it.

Romans 8:12–14 (NIV84) 12 Therefore, brothers, we have an obligation—but it is not to the sinful nature, to live according to it. 13 For if you live according to the sinful nature, you will die; but if by the Spirit you put to death the misdeeds of the body, you will live, 14 because those who are led by the Spirit of God are sons of God.

Just as a doctor uses medical tests to determine the condition of a patient, Romans 7 and 8 can be used as a test to know if we just have a head knowledge about Christianity or if we are truly Born of the Spirit of God. The one born of the Spirit has the desire to walk with God and his commands are not burdensome. (I John 5:3) The one Born of God has the Spirit within him that wars against the fleshly nature and make the nature of God alive.

1 John 3:7–10 (NIV84) 7 Dear children, do not let anyone lead you astray. He who does what is right is righteous, just as he is righteous. 8 He who does what is sinful is of the devil, because the devil has been sinning from the beginning. The

reason the Son of God appeared was to destroy the devil's work. 9 No one who is born of God will continue to sin, because God's seed remains in him; he cannot go on sinning, because he has been born of God. 10 This is how we know who the children of God are and who the children of the devil are: Anyone who does not do what is right is not a child of God; nor is anyone who does not love his brother.

That's why Jesus didn't say that you would know them by their confession of faith, but instead said, "You will know them by their fruit." The fruit of the Holy Spirit of God as outlined in Galatians 5. It is not of works; it is the Spirit of Grace bringing out the Fruit of the Spirit and changing people's lives from the inside out. Take the test of 2 Corinthians 13:5 (NIV84) "Examine yourselves to see whether you are in the faith; test yourselves. Do you not realize that Christ Jesus is in you—unless, of course, you fail the test?"

If you have not asked the Spirit of Christ to come into your life, He is a free gift, you cannot do enough to earn his work in your life. Open you heart to the words of Jesus himself,

Luke 11:11–13 (NIV84) 11 "Which of you fathers, if your son asks for a fish, will give him a snake instead? 12 Or if he asks for an egg, will give him a scorpion? 13 If you then, though you are evil, know how to give good gifts to your children, how much more will your Father in heaven give the Holy Spirit to those who ask him!"

Ask the Holy Spirit into your heart today and may the Grace of God work mightily within you as you walk with him.

THREE TOUCHSTONES OF TRUTH

Introduction:

Jesus said that the true worshipers will worship is Spirit and in Truth. It takes both to be true spirituality. If only the Word is focused on spirituality can become only an academic mental exercise. Knowing truth becomes more important than acting on it. If only the Spirit is focused on, they can lose connection with the head, which is Jesus Christ, the Word of God. Both the Work of the Holy Spirit and the Word of God are needed for true spirituality. But how are we to know what is true? There are three touchstones that we need to be familiar with as Christians.

Three Touchstones:

1st The Word of God:

There are some "versions" of the Bible out there that we should be weary of; those that are translated by a single author or denomination. But if you use an international / interdenominational translation there have been checks and balances, put in place to remain true to the Hebrew, Aramaic, and Greek texts. Read the preface of the Bible you use to know how it came into being; It's important.

Also recognize that the notes that are included in study Bibles reflect the beliefs of one man or denomination. Get into the Word of God and study it for yourself and the light of God and Christ will enter your heart.

2nd The Work of the Holy Spirit:

The Apostle John instructed the saints to test the spirit, because everything that is done in the name of the Holy Spirit is not of him.

> 1 John 4:1 (NIV84) Dear friends, do not believe every spirit, but test the spirits to see whether they are from God, because many false prophets have gone out into the world.

John goes on to speak of an issue in his say and that was there were those who didn't believe that Jesus came in a body of flesh, but in a spiritual body. John proclaimed this as coming from the antichrist. In like manner there are those who attribute to the Holy Spirit actions that counter the work of the Holy Spirit. The work of the Holy Spirit is laid out in God's Word.

1. He is one that is called alongside as a comforter and counselor. (John 14:15-31)

2. He opposes following the fleshly nature and promotes a Godly lifestyle. (Galatians 5:16-18)

3. He works the Gifts of the Spirit in the ministries of the Called. (I Corinthians 2:6-16, Chapter 12-14)

4. He instills the Fruit of the Spirit in the hearts and lives of the Called. (Galatians 5:19-26)

The Spirit is like the Father and the Son. Jesus told his disciples that anyone who has seen him has seen the Father. In Like manner Jesus told his disciple that he would send them another counselor, the promised Holy Spirit. In the Greek language there are two words for "Another": another or other of the same kind or another of a different kind. Jesus said he was sending another of the same kind as himself. Paul was concerned with people being deceived into believing another Gospel, receiving a different Jesus or Spirit.

2 Corinthians 11:3–4 (NIV84) 3 But I am afraid that just as Eve was deceived by the serpent's cunning, your minds may somehow be led astray from your sincere and pure devotion to Christ. 4 For if someone comes to you and preaches a Jesus other than the Jesus we preached, or if you receive a different spirit from the one you received, or a different gospel from the one you accepted, you put up with it easily enough.

Whenever the Spirit was poured out the people declared the Glories of God (Acts 2) and proclaimed the Word of God with Great boldness along with a call for God to perform miraculous confirmations (Acts 4:29-30). But also, Jesus corrected those who were always looking for a sign or a miraculous act. Spirituality can become superficial when focusing on experiences to the extent that the mission of proclaiming the Word of God gets lost in the process.

When manifestations become an end in themselves spirituality becomes shallow and superficial. The receiver feels their excitement and response is the goal rather than an equipping for service amid opposition and suffering. This is the difference between the Pentecostal and the Charismatic viewpoints. Pentecostals focus on the infilling of the Spirit and the receiving of the Gifts as an equipping for service, while the Charismatics focus on their own personal edification. In the Church the focus should be on the building of the whole.

In my life experience the Holy Spirit has most often spoke to me by bringing to my mind the Word of God. The Rama, the Spoken Word, points to the Logos, the Written Word. There is safety in this process because the Rama always has a source of confirmation. Those who want to speak outside the realm of the Written Word are in danger of great error, and what they say must be tested against the Character of the Word of God, against the Character and work of the Spirit, and finally against the life of Christ, the only truly spiritual person.

3rd The Life of Christ:

Jesus' life is the third touchstone for true spirituality. Jesus had the Spirit without measure (John 3:34) and didn't display a strange manifestation even once. The Holy Spirit does not possess us, we remain in control, he abides with us doing his work of sanctification, purification, and empowerment. Taking a long look at Jesus' life shows us what the Spirit Filled Life is supposed to look like. Those who are seeking ecstatic experiences over an obedient life walk are on a spiritually dangerous road which leads into the realm of false prophets.

I am for the Work of the Spirit in mine and people's lives. I want everything the Lord wants to give to me, but I'm going to test the Spirit to see if they are truly in line with the character of the Word, The Spirit and Jesus' life. As it says in Ecclesiastes 7:18 (NIV84) … The man who fears God will avoid all extremes.

A QUANTUM LEAP IN ILLOGIC.

For years efforts have been made to blur Male and Female Roles. In dress there was the attempt to create the Metrosexual that looked neither male nor female. The women's movement has moved from equal rights to sameness. There are legitimate needs for women to have equal rights, such as in pay for the same level of work, but when they are taken beyond equality to sameness; not seeing any difference between a man and woman things take place that goes against God's Kingdom and his creation. There are also creator rights and when we think our desires and wants supersedes His decrees it is called sin.

Let's take a little walk-through history. In the 1950's the vast majority of women worked in or out of the home. Those that did work outside the home were not in manual labor. Most women worked in secretarial or support roles. Then came along World War II and the need for Rosie the Riveter. Women left the home in record numbers to help the War effort. When the war ended, many did not return to the home and the invention of the latch key kid was born. Today we see a woman in military uniform carrying a rifle in Iraq and the roles of men and women have been mixed. This blurring of the roles has led people into a world view that contradicts God desire that there be a distinction between the Sexes. Even in dress.

Deuteronomy 22:5 (NIV84) 5 A woman must not wear men's clothing, nor a man wear women's clothing, for the LORD your God detests anyone who does this.

That leads us to Washington State's SB6239, same sex marriage law. The Assemblies of God has provided information to its Ministers concerning the Legal changes being made.

In a related move, the 9th U.S. Circuit Court of Appeals concurred on February 8th that the 2008 California referendum (Prop. 8) banning same-sex marriage is indeed unconstitutional, upholding a decision by U.S. District Judge Vaughn Walker who had ruled Proposition 8 unconstitutional last year. Walker noted in his decision that although it was passed by 52% of the vote, the outcome is "irrelevant" because "fundamental rights may not be submitted to a vote." Additionally, Walker wrote in his decision that "moral disapproval alone is an improper basis on which to deny rights to gay men and women." He is also quoted as saying that marriage is "an artifact of a time when the genders were seen as having distinct roles in society and in marriage-that time has passed."

Notice the sequence in Illogic:

1) Since Women are involved in every type and kind of labor in the workplace…

2) Since men and women share the duties of the Home and there is no longer role distinctions…

3) Therefore, it doesn't matter if the family is made up of two men or two women instead of the traditional man and wife.

4) The women's movement is being used to justify and legalize homosexual relationships and marriage.

Mankind is always looking for ways to justify their sin, but Jesus made an interesting statement about those who promote what God calls sin.

Matthew 18:5–7 (NIV84) 5 "And whoever welcomes a little child like this in my name welcomes me. 6 But if anyone causes one of these little ones who believe in me to sin, it would be better for him to have a large millstone hung around his neck and to be drowned in the depths of the sea. 7 "Woe to the world because of the things that cause people to sin! Such things must come, but woe to the man through whom they come!

I agree and want women to be treated fairly, but to destroy the roles completely leads people into lifestyle that will keep them out of the Kingdom of God. And lead them to judgment also for promoting sin in people's lives.

Quote from email sent out by Don Detrick, Secretary/Treasurer NW District of the Assemblies of God states:

"Clearly, a biblical view of marriage is being challenged in America. How should we respond? While the words of Walker and others stir our emotions and seem poised to deconstruct the basic fabric of western civilization, perhaps the best defense of traditional marriage is for the church to provide a healthy model of such.
By doing nothing we can be subtly be moving as a Nation into the process of depravity that will destroy us. Please take to heart the words of Romans 1:18-32."

Romans 1:18–32 (NIV84) 18 The wrath of God is being revealed from heaven against all the godlessness and wickedness of men who suppress the truth by their wickedness, 19 since what may be known about God is plain to them, because God has made it plain to them. 20 For since the creation of the world God's invisible qualities—his eternal power and divine nature—have been clearly seen, being understood from what has been made, so that men are without excuse.

21 For although they knew God, they neither glorified him as God nor gave thanks to him, but their thinking became futile and their foolish hearts were darkened. 22 Although

they claimed to be wise, they became fools 23 and exchanged the glory of the immortal God for images made to look like mortal man and birds and animals and reptiles.

24 Therefore God gave them over in the sinful desires of their hearts to sexual impurity for the degrading of their bodies with one another. 25 They exchanged the truth of God for a lie, and worshiped and served created things rather than the Creator—who is forever praised. Amen.

26 Because of this, God gave them over to shameful lusts. Even their women exchanged natural relations for unnatural ones. 27 In the same way the men also abandoned natural relations with women and were inflamed with lust for one another. Men committed indecent acts with other men, and received in themselves the due penalty for their perversion.

28 Furthermore, since they did not think it worthwhile to retain the knowledge of God, he gave them over to a depraved mind, to do what ought not to be done. 29 They have become filled with every kind of wickedness, evil, greed and depravity. They are full of envy, murder, strife, deceit and malice. They are gossips, 30 slanderers, God-haters, insolent, arrogant and boastful; they invent ways of doing evil; they disobey their parents; 31 they are senseless, faithless, heartless, ruthless. 32 Although they know God's righteous decree that those who do such things deserve death, they not only continue to do these very things but also approve of those who practice them.

I have been told that a Bible is being produced that reflects the beliefs of the Culture where Homosexuality is approved. Our Culture and laws do not determine the culture and Laws of the Kingdom of God. Christianity is based on the Character of God not the whims of people. Regardless, of Society's shifts, God has given Men and Women roles to fulfill. Regardless of the shift of our nation's politics the Kingdom of God stands firm. Jesus said, "I am the way, the truth and the life. No one comes to the Father except through me." Those who wish to be Men and women of God will search His Word to find out what the Characteristics of a Man of God and a Woman of God are. They will want to be the Husbands and Wives that God's Word proclaims and the kind of parents that He expects. Read the Word and get it down into your Spirit and Soul and Bones until the Fire and Passion of the Lord burns within you. Then you will find the Kingdom of God and the indwelling of His Spirit.

> Jeremiah 20:9 (NIV84) Jeremiah's Complaint
> 9 But if I say, "I will not mention him
> or speak any more in his name,"
> his Word is in my heart like a fire,
> a fire shut up in my bones.
> I am weary of holding it in;
> indeed, I cannot

Hunger for that fire as it will burn into eternal life. Christians rise up! You are called to be Men and Women of God: Search His Word to discover His Roles and gifts for your Life. We are God's Ambassadors and need to represent our King not our or the world's desires.

THE LOVE OF GOD

The phrase the love of God is an interesting statement because it can mean God's love for us or our love for God. The fact of the matter is that the Love of God always begins with God. He loved us first. No one can come to him unless he draws us to himself. Jesus made that clear in His teaching. God's love is consistent. People's love fluctuates. We can love the Lord but love sin more and be focusing on forgiveness rather than obedience.

People who focus on faith tell me that I was already saved because I believed. I was sprinkled Methodist, Confirmed Lutheran, convicted Baptist and saved Assembly of God. They all assumed that by teaching me their doctrines that I was saved. But you can know a lot about the things of God and still not love Him. I had gained a lot of knowledge; I knew about God the Father and Jesus, but I didn't love him enough to truly turn to him. It wasn't until I was 25 years old that I started to think about applying what I knew to my life and started to desire to be obedient. I look back now and see that God started leading me from the point I chose to Love him and he led me right into the place where I could receive him. This corresponds to what Jesus taught.

> John 14:15–24 (NIV84) 15 "If you love me, you will obey what I command. 16 And I will ask the Father, and he will give you another Counselor to be with you forever— 17 the Spirit of truth. The world cannot accept him, because it neither sees him nor knows him. But you know him, for he lives with you and will be in you. 18 I will not leave you as orphans; I will come to you. 19 Before long, the world will not see me anymore, but you will see me. Because I live, you also will

live. 20 On that day you will realize that I am in my Father, and you are in me, and I am in you. 21 Whoever has my commands and obeys them, he is the one who loves me. He who loves me will be loved by my Father, and I too will love him and show myself to him."

22 Then Judas (not Judas Iscariot) said, "But, Lord, why do you intend to show yourself to us and not to the world?"

23 Jesus replied, "If anyone loves me, he will obey my teaching. My Father will love him, and we will come to him and make our home with him. 24 He who does not love me will not obey my teaching. These words you hear are not my own; they belong to the Father who sent me.

I love the Church, but too often leaders start to think that by believing their Doctrinal positions a person is saved. Church leaders want to make things simple and often make doctrines of salvation that negate the teaching of Christ. It's not by faith alone. Coming into a loving relationship with Christ through His Spirit will affect every area of your live. Faith is just the conduit that takes you to the grace of a transformed and converted life. Ministers can proclaim someone saved who show no evidence of conversion. Jesus didn't say that you would know them by their confession of faith but by their fruit. As the Apostle Paul said,

> I Corinthians 7:19 (NIV84) 19 Circumcision is nothing and uncircumcision is nothing. Keeping God's commands is what counts.

> Galatians 6:15 (NIV84) 15 Neither circumcision nor uncircumcision means anything; what counts is a new creation.

These two passages together say the same thing that Jesus did. Obey Jesus' commands and teachings and it leads to becoming a New Creation in Christ.

We can take on beliefs that make us comfortable with the world, and the world comfortable with us, and thereby find our teachings in conflict with the Words of Christ. We can also be relying on God's forgiveness rather than hungering and thirsting after righteousness because we love sin more than the Lord.

Don't judge anyone else's heart but take a strong look at your own. Do you love the Lord and his teaching? If you do you will find the Spirit of God working within you to bring about His character and holiness. There has never been a revival where Holiness wasn't increased as well. Because the Spirit is Holy.

> Galatians 5:16–18 (NIV84) 16 So I say, live by the Spirit, and you will not gratify the desires of the sinful nature. 17 For the sinful nature desires what is contrary to the Spirit, and the Spirit what is contrary to the sinful nature. They are in conflict with each other, so that you do not do what you want. 18 But if you are led by the Spirit, you are not under law.

Jesus is not an excuse for wicked living, He is the reason for a transformed and converted life. Seek the Love of the Lord. It is available to those who obey Him!

HEAD AND HEART KNOWLEDGE.

Belief is not knowing. That is really a very profound thought. But a critical one in the Christian faith. You can believe a lot of truth and still not come to a place of knowing it from personal experience. Here are some examples; I have seen Doctors and Nurses standing outside the Hospital smoking. They believe that smoking is bad for you but they haven't really come to own it through knowing from personal experience. Belief in the facts that they have stuck in their heads have not reached to their hearts where they really know the truth. A couple of passages show that Jesus and the Apostles proclaimed this truth also.

> John 5:39–40 (NIV84) 39 You diligently study the Scriptures because you think that by them you possess eternal life. These are the Scriptures that testify about me, 40 yet you refuse to come to me to have life.

> 2 Timothy 3:6–7 (NIV84) 6 They are the kind who worm their way into homes and gain control over weak-willed women, who are loaded down with sins and are swayed by all kinds of evil desires, 7 always learning but never able to acknowledge the truth.

It has always been amazing to me to see people who know a lot of spiritual truth but it hasn't made it to their hearts, and I know because I did it for 25 years; you see it with the heart one comes to be saved and out of the abundance of the heart the mouth speaks.

Head knowledge doesn't change actions, but heart knowledge does.

Those who know about the Lord just have a knowledge sitting in their brains, but those who repent and surrender their lives to Christ receive the Holy Spirit who works from within to confirm and promote the Word of God in their lives. That is why Jesus didn't say you will know them by their confession of faith, but that you would know them by their fruit; what their life produces. The Apostle Paul explained this:

> 1 Corinthians 2:10–16 (NIV84) 10 but God has revealed it to us by his Spirit.
>
> The Spirit searches all things, even the deep things of God. 11 For who among men knows the thoughts of a man except the man's spirit within him? In the same way no one knows the thoughts of God except the Spirit of God. 12 We have not received the spirit of the world but the Spirit who is from God, that we may understand what God has freely given us. 13 This is what we speak, not in words taught us by human wisdom but in words taught by the Spirit, expressing spiritual truths in spiritual words. 14 The man without the Spirit does not accept the things that come from the Spirit of God, for they are foolishness to him, and he cannot understand them, because they are spiritually discerned. 15 The spiritual man makes judgments about all things, but he himself is not subject to any man's judgment:
>
> 16   "For who has known the mind of the Lord
>
> that he may instruct him?"
>
> But we have the mind of Christ.

Those who love the Lord will obey him and he will come into their hearts and open their eyes and ears to the truth of his Word. Seek and call upon the Lord Jesus today and turn from your ways and Hunger after the fullness of His Spirit in your life and rich blessing await you. If you are ready to do this today, you can pray this prayer and Jesus will see your heart and respond:

Lord Jesus, I need to know you and be forgiven the sins of my heart. Cleans me today and come into my life and lead me and teach me as I read your Word found in the Bible. I will continue to seek you until I know you have heard me and come into my heart for, I want your life to live in me. I ask this in your name. Amen

It is my prayer that God will bless you richly as you seek him today and continue to do so. If you prayed this prayer, please find a Full Gospel Church that will help you grown in Christ Jesus.

PERSONAL REVIVAL

The passage I'm about to share I used a bit ago, but the Spirit of the Lord has been continuing to speak to me about it. Real, Lasting, revival begins and endures on the personal level. A major public revival begins when a large group of people do these things all at the same time. Judas, not Judas Iscariot, asked Jesus the most important question of all time. I call it the Question of Evangelism and Revival. He asked, "But, Lord, why do you intend to show yourself to us and not to the world?" Real, Lasting Revival begins with a true vision of who God is. His life is what changes our lives. Jesus' presence in someone's life was the Test the Apostle Paul considered the critical one. He said so in 2 Corinthians 13:5 (NIV84)

> 5 Examine yourselves to see whether you are in the faith; test yourselves. Do you not realize that Christ Jesus is in you —unless, of course, you fail the test?

People focus on faith, but true faith leads to a relationship with the Lord that is in accordance with His Word. Jesus said, …

John 14:15–24 (NIV84) 15 "If you love me, you will obey what I command. 16 And I will ask the Father, and he will give you another Counselor to be with you forever— 17 the Spirit of truth. The world cannot accept him, because it neither sees him nor knows him. But you know him, for he lives with you and will be in you. 18 I will not leave you as orphans; I will come to you. 19 Before long, the world will not see me anymore, but you will see me. Because I live, you also will live. 20 On that day you will realize that I am in my Father, and you are in me, and I am in you. 21 Whoever has my commands and obeys them, he is the one who loves me. He who loves me will be loved by my Father, and I too will love him and show myself to him."

22 Then Judas (not Judas Iscariot) said, "But, Lord, why do you intend to show yourself to us and not to the world?"

23 Jesus replied, "If anyone loves me, he will obey my teaching. My Father will love him, and we will come to him and make our home with him. 24 He who does not love me will not obey my teaching. These words you hear are not my own; they belong to the Father who sent me.

Many people consider themselves Christians and think Jesus thinks like they do, but we need to test our thinking and read the Words and Teaching of Christ in the Gospels to see if our thinking is in line with His, not just assume He thinks like we do. If you have a Bible where the Words of Christ are in Red do a Bible study with the express purpose of looking for what Jesus liked and disliked. What he taught about life here on this planet and ask yourself do I really love God's ways. Here is an important statement; You can know and believe a lot of things Jesus said but not love His ways. What you love you will live out and Jesus didn't say that he would come to those who believed but to those who loved His Words and Teachings.

You want personal and corporate Revival, start loving the Things Jesus loved and put them into practice and you will find Jesus' Spirit moving into your life and making Himself at home there, That is a revival of the soul.

JESUS' LOVE LANGUAGE

Dr. Gary Chapman, Christian counselor and author of The Five Love Languages writes about how to express love to your mate. Not everyone has the same love language. You may be showing love in your language, but it does not translate into love in your mate's language. Dr. Chapman's Five Love Languages are Words of Affirmation, Quality Time, Gifts, Acts of Service and Physical Touch.

But what is God's Love Language? Being God, His is not one of the Five that Dr. Chapman writes about. God's Love Language is clearly Obedience. This is true of God the Father and God the Son and God the Holy Spirit which can be grieved through disobedience. And there are many illustrations of people trying to show love in a different language and God proclaiming it false.

Some illustrations of false love being shown to God; King Saul Disobeying by providing a sacrifice to God. God wants obedience, not sacrifice.

1 Samuel 13:7–14 (NIV84) 7 Some Hebrews even crossed the Jordan to the land of Gad and Gilead. Saul remained at Gilgal, and all the troops with him were quaking with fear. 8 He waited seven days, the time set by Samuel; but Samuel did not come to Gilgal, and Saul's men began to scatter. 9 So he said, "Bring me the burnt offering and the fellowship offerings." And Saul offered up the burnt offering. 10 Just as he finished making the offering, Samuel arrived, and Saul

went out to greet him.

11 "What have you done?" asked Samuel.

Saul replied, "When I saw that the men were scattering, and that you did not come at the set time, and that the Philistines were assembling at Micmash, 12 I thought, 'Now the Philistines will come down against me at Gilgal, and I have not sought the LORD's favor.' So I felt compelled to offer the burnt offering."

13 "You acted foolishly," Samuel said. "You have not kept the command the LORD your God gave you; if you had, he would have established your kingdom over Israel for all time. 14 But now your kingdom will not endure; the LORD has sought out a man after his own heart and appointed him leader of his people, because you have not kept the LORD's command."

God, speaking through the prophet Hosea said these words, Hosea 6:6 (NIV84) 6 For I desire mercy, not sacrifice, and acknowledgment of God rather than burnt offerings.

Jesus repeated the first part of this in Matthew 9:13 & 12:7. And King David recognized this also when he penned the words of Psalm 51.

Psalm 51:16–17 (NIV84)

16 You do not delight in sacrifice, or I would bring it;

you do not take pleasure in burnt offerings.

17 The sacrifices of God are a broken spirit;

a broken and contrite heart,

O God, you will not despise.

But more importantly Jesus has proclaimed His love Language in a number of ways, and they all speak of obedience.

John 14:15–24 (NIV84) 15 "If you love me, you will obey what I command. 16 And I will ask the Father, and he will give you another Counselor to be with you forever— 17 the Spirit of

> truth. The world cannot accept him, because it neither sees him nor knows him. But you know him, for he lives with you and will be in you. 18 I will not leave you as orphans; I will come to you. 19 Before long, the world will not see me anymore, but you will see me. Because I live, you also will live. 20 On that day you will realize that I am in my Father, and you are in me, and I am in you. 21 Whoever has my commands and obeys them, he is the one who loves me. He who loves me will be loved by my Father, and I too will love him and show myself to him."
>
> 22 Then Judas (not Judas Iscariot) said, "But, Lord, why do you intend to show yourself to us and not to the world?"
>
> 23 Jesus replied, "If anyone loves me, he will obey my teaching. My Father will love him, and we will come to him and make our home with him. 24 He who does not love me will not obey my teaching. These words you hear are not my own; they belong to the Father who sent me.

And again, in Luke 6 Jesus speaks the need for obedience.

> Luke 6:46–49 (NIV84) 46 "Why do you call me, 'Lord, Lord,' and do not do what I say? 47 I will show you what he is like who comes to me and hears my words and puts them into practice. 48 He is like a man building a house, who dug down deep and laid the foundation on rock. When a flood came, the torrent struck that house but could not shake it, because it was well built. 49 But the one who hears my words and does not put them into practice is like a man who built a house on the ground without a foundation. The moment the torrent struck that house, it collapsed and its destruction was complete."

There are hundreds of other examples in the scriptures. Obedience is God's love language. Jesus came to save and has and is showing great love and longsuffering, but when he returns it will be to judge, please do not be one of those who ignore the Word of God for a walk with God is a sure foundation and the blessed hope.

ABOUT THE AUTHOR

Stephen Mandeville

Stephen Mandeville grew up on the Olympic Peninsula in Washington State. Served in the U.S. Army in Germany. He graduated with a BA in Pastoral Ministry fron Northwest College, now Northwest University in 1981. Pioneered Quilcene Assembly and was an Associate Pastor at Lighthouse Christian Center in Port Angeles, WA. He has been in ministry with the Assemblies of God for over 40 years. He has a wife, Ellen, and three children, Leah, Joshua and Nathan and eight grandchildren. "I am Blessed".
Webpage: http://mandeville-wordcraft.com
email: contact@mandeville-wordcraft.com

BOOKS BY THIS AUTHOR

The Called Out Ones Series

The Called Out Ones Series Everywhere the Apostle Paul went there were riots and revival. Revolutionary, Thought Provoking, Life Changing, Biblical, Jesus. This book could have the same effect. "Mandeville Wordcraft" on Facebook.

Webpage: http://mandeville-wordcraft.com
email: contact@mandeville-wordcraft.com

Made in the USA
Middletown, DE
01 July 2024